DECORATIVE
FRAMES

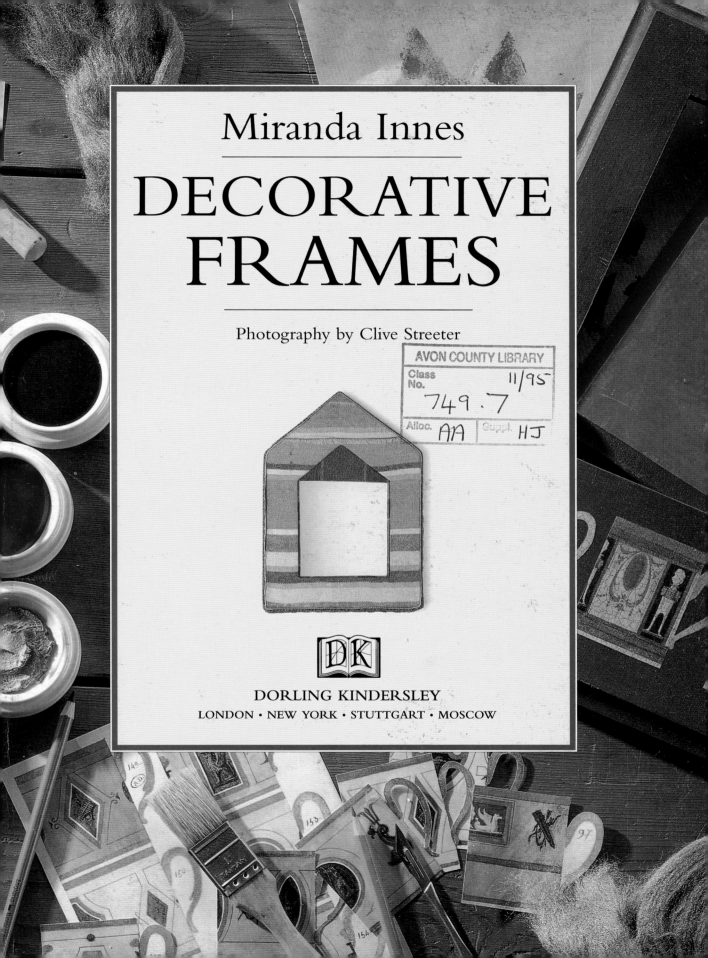

Miranda Innes

DECORATIVE FRAMES

Photography by Clive Streeter

DK

DORLING KINDERSLEY

LONDON · NEW YORK · STUTTGART · MOSCOW

A DORLING KINDERSLEY BOOK

Created and produced by
COLLINS & BROWN LIMITED
London House
Great Eastern Wharf
Parkgate Road
London SW11 4NQ

Project Editor	Heather Dewhurst
Managing Editor	Sarah Hoggett
Editorial Assistant	Corinne Asghar
Art Director	Roger Bristow
Art Editor	Marnie Searchwell
DTP Designer	Claire Graham
Design Assistant	David Drew
Photography	Clive Streeter
Stylist	Ali Edney

First published in Great Britain in 1995
by Dorling Kindersley Limited
9 Henrietta Street, London WC2E 8PS

A CIP catalogue record for this book is available
from the British Library.

ISBN 0 7513 0248 1

Reproduced by Colourscan, Malaysia
Printed and bound in France by Pollina - n° 67508 - B

Contents

Wood and Metal Frames

Paper and Fabric Frames

Introduction

FRAMES are a decorator's dream: they make your works of art feel at home; they elevate undistinguished prints into something noteworthy; they can make a motley collection of fond memorabilia take on a more dignified form; and, if they are surrounding a mirror, they make a flattering foil for your face.

Frames work in a room rather like jewellery or accessories; strong, matching or harmonizing frames can echo a colour scheme or highlight motifs from the existing decor, bringing together all the elements like a musical fugue. If you do not possess quite enough courage to call yourself an artist or painter as such, you can always sidle surreptitiously towards being one by surrounding your still life with a frame that emphasizes its colours, shapes, and even the objects themselves, so that the whole will be emphatically greater than the sum of its

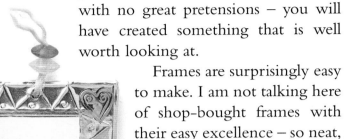

Foil Finesse
Humble components assembled with dash for a jewel of a frame.

parts. Without too much effort – and with no great pretensions – you will have created something that is well worth looking at.

Frames are surprisingly easy to make. I am not talking here of shop-bought frames with their easy excellence – so neat, predictable and bland, that you do not actually see them at all. This book is full of frames that you can make yourself and embellish upon, frames with character, charm and relevance to your own life, of which you can be justifiably proud. If your finished frame engulfs the print you made it for, so what? Chuck away the print, put a mirror in the frame in its place and bask in glorious reflections.

To make a frame you need little in the way of raw materials, just a few lengths of cheap timber or even cardboard, and some paint, paper, fabric and glue. You will find most of the more interesting ingredients around your home, lying unused in drawers or scrap bags. You might be galvanized into action by a significant birthday, a new baby,

Waterworks
A watercolour seascape perfectly moored amid driftwood.

Kindest Cuts
Copy, cut and colour – the photocopier is your friend.

or your parents' wedding anniversary. All those cards and beautiful wrapping paper, the ribbons and the roses – too full of memories to throw away – might persuade you to arrange them tentatively on a sheet of delicate handmade paper. If your collage is successful, you might then feel encouraged to do it credit with a frame rich with découpage cut from the wrapping paper, or a papier mâché frame made from the bright tissue that packaged the champagne glasses.

Rhythm in Blue
Elegant Italianate lettering adorns a papier mâché frame.

Beautifully framed memories are so much more meaningful than photos and cards stuffed in a bag at the back of a cupboard.

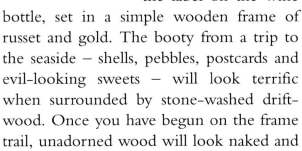

Scrap Happy
Curvaceous shape in card covered in rich cloth.

All sorts of things benefit from being dressed up in this way – you can remind yourself of a blissful time in the country with a collage of photos, autumn leaves, the bill for dinner and the label on the wine bottle, set in a simple wooden frame of russet and gold. The booty from a trip to the seaside – shells, pebbles, postcards and evil-looking sweets – will look terrific when surrounded by stone-washed driftwood. Once you have begun on the frame trail, unadorned wood will look naked and unfinished. Your fingers will itch to transform all those unadventurous rectangles around your home with a spot of gilding, a flight of stencils, or a subtle and seductive wood stain.

Ready-made frames are cheap, and save trouble and time as a basis for your creative flurries. Let someone else go to the trouble of cutting perfect mitres that do not fall apart – you have more interesting things to do. Such as having a go at mosaic. You probably always thought, wrongly, that huge expertise was required. But not a bit of it, just a simple idea and plenty of patience. Once you have experimented with glorious glittering tesserae bought from a shop, you might go on to recycle the shattered remnants of your beautiful blue and white Spode dinner service. Or you might undertake an adventure in kitsch, using fragments of a mirror and glass gems from a bead shop.

All sorts of things go into making frames, and frames can be made from all sorts of things. With this book and a dash of ingenuity, splendid surroundings are yours for the making.

Regal Rags
Hand-hooked from scraps – a recycler's crowning glory.

7

Basic Techniques and Finishes

To make a good picture frame you need the right tools and equipment. The essential tools are: craft knife, metal ruler, tenon saw and mitre box, clamps, hanging fittings and nylon cord. You will also need these materials: wooden moulding, mountboard, PVA glue, gummed parcel tape, glass cut to size, and hardboard for backing.

Measuring and making a frame

First decide on the size of your frame. Measure the length and width of the picture or mount, if any, then add on 3mm (⅛in) to each measurement to allow for fitting. Add the two measurements and multiply this figure by 2 to give you the total length. To allow for moulding projecting beyond the picture at the corners, multiply the width of the moulding by 8 and add this to the total. Finally, add on 5cm (2in) to allow for cutting. This figure is the total length of moulding you should buy. It is best to buy moulding in one length rather than two, in case there are slight discrepancies in their manufacture.

Accurate measuring is vital when cutting the pieces of the frame. Always measure along the outside edge of the moulding to find the point to cut. The length of each side of the frame, therefore, should be the length or width of the picture plus 3mm (⅛in), plus twice the moulding width.

Each piece of the frame should have a mitred corner running in opposite directions. Check as you go that you are cutting the pieces correctly. After mitring the corners, do not sand them, even though the edges might feel rough, as they will not fit together properly. Leave any sanding until the frame has been assembled. For extra reinforcement you can hammer two panel pins into each corner.

Decide how much of the picture you want to show, then add 5-7.5cm (2-3in) for the mount borders. Cut out the mount for the picture using a craft knife or mount cutters. Cutting a bevelled edge may take a bit of practice; using mount cutters makes the job easier. They have the blade set at the right angle and it is adjustable to accommodate different thicknesses of mountboard.

Finishing the frame

To hang the picture, screw in the hanging hooks in each side of the frame, about a third of the way down from the top. Then tie nylon cord across the back, making sure it is neither completely taut, nor so slack that the cord will be seen above the top of the frame.

Once you have made your picture frame, you can either leave it as it is with the wood-grain visible, or use one or more paints to produce an interesting finish, a range of which is illustrated below.

◄ *Fine, even lines are produced by pulling a long-haired brush through wet glaze.*

◄ *This frame was stained around a stencil and the resulting pattern outlined in black paint.*

◄ *A verdigris effect is achieved by sponging mint-green paint over a dark greyish base, then sponging gold paint sparingly on top.*

◄ *This repetitive stencilled pattern was painted in gold on a black ground. The paintwork was rubbed back to age it.*

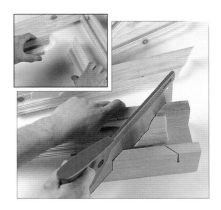

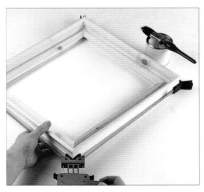

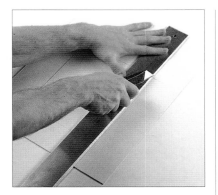

1 *Holding the moulding in the mitre box, saw one edge to a mitre running in the right direction. Measure the length of the frame. Cut the second mitred corner so that it runs in the opposite direction. Cut three more lengths. Glue the mitred ends together (see inset).*

2 *Place the frame in a clamp to hold the sides together. The best type has three L-shaped corner brackets and a fourth adjustable bracket with nylon tape running around all the sides. Place the corner brackets on, tighten the tape and leave the frame in a clamp overnight.*

3 *Draw the dimensions of the mount on the reverse of a piece of mountboard. Holding a metal ruler along the outer line as a guide, cut along the line with a craft knife in one fluid movement. Cut the mount window holding the knife at an angle of about 60° for a bevelled edge.*

4 *Tape the picture to the reverse of the mount. Assemble the frame by inserting the glass cut to size, then the mount and picture, face down, then hardboard cut to size for the backing. Hammer small nails into the sides of the frame to secure (see inset).*

5 *Stick gummed parcel tape around the edges of the hardboard and the frame to keep out dust and moisture. Using a bradawl to make holes in the wood, screw two hanging hooks into the sides of the frame. Tie nylon cord across the back and knot securely.*

6 *The frame is now complete. Check that the hanging cord is not visible from the front and hang the picture on the wall.*

◄ *Pull a comb through wet glaze for a striped pattern.*

◄ *Several paint glazes are applied onto a surface and softened to produce faux tortoise-shell.*

◄ *Stencilling is one of the most effective paint techniques.*

► *This variation of the combing technique produces an interesting wavy pattern.*

► *Ragging over a strongly coloured wet glaze produces lively patterns.*

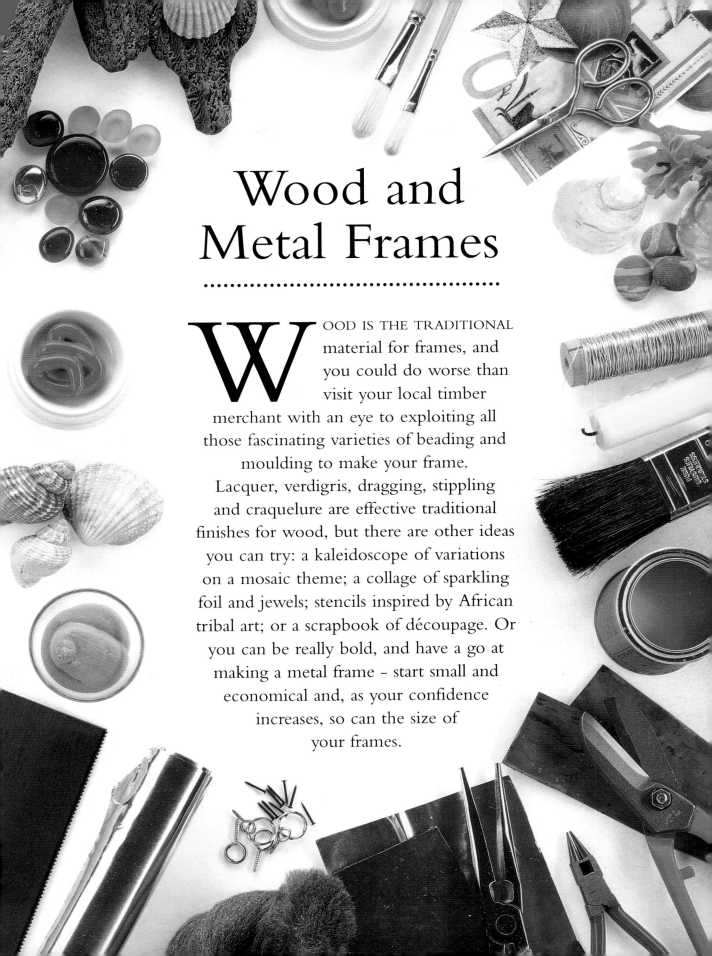

Wood and Metal Frames

·······································

WOOD IS THE TRADITIONAL material for frames, and you could do worse than visit your local timber merchant with an eye to exploiting all those fascinating varieties of beading and moulding to make your frame. Lacquer, verdigris, dragging, stippling and craquelure are effective traditional finishes for wood, but there are other ideas you can try: a kaleidoscope of variations on a mosaic theme; a collage of sparkling foil and jewels; stencils inspired by African tribal art; or a scrapbook of découpage. Or you can be really bold, and have a go at making a metal frame – start small and economical and, as your confidence increases, so can the size of your frames.

Antiquated Paper

MATERIALS

Wooden frame
Red acrylic emulsion paint
Candle
Green acrylic emulsion paint
Decorative paper motifs
PVA glue
Water-based craquelure (two solutions)
Raw umber artist's oil colour

EQUIPMENT

Sandpaper
Artist's brush
Wire wool
Scalpel
Cutting mat
Small nail scissors
Paper towels
Cloth

NOTHING BEATS DECOUPAGE for quick and easy effectiveness, and it provides an instant way to jazz up a plain wooden frame. We are surrounded by images begging to be snipped from magazines, wrapping paper, greetings cards and catalogues, and recycled as part of our own personal memorabilia. Tickets, invitations, fond messages scribbled on the corner of a newspaper – these can all do duty in this magpie art. With découpage you can be clever, witty, nostalgic or pretty – the choice is yours. Try to ensure that there are common denominators of colour to help marry image and background. Likewise, having a textured background will prevent your découpage motif from standing out too glaringly.

Careful cutting is all important in découpage – tiny curved nail scissors can manage tricky curves while a scalpel will make light work of the rest. Remember that scalpels are used for surgery and are lethally sharp, and use a cutting mat or piece of cardboard to protect your work surface.

Ruff and Scumble

Marie Vignon, this splendidly bedecked figure, presides with a coy smile over a Tudor snack. The dark and distressed red and green of the frame is close in tone to the portrait, and the graphic refinement of the Napoleonic coffee cans parallels that of the finely detailed ruff and bodice.

Découpage Decoration

Photocopied engravings can be aged in tea or painted with watercolour. The chunky vegetables taken from ancient seed-packets would make an appropriate frame for the award of merit at your local flower show. Découpage is a great opportunity to co-ordinate picture with frame.

Decorating the Frame

The joy of découpage is that it is very easy to do, you know what it will look like and with very little effort you can produce something convincingly sophisticated.

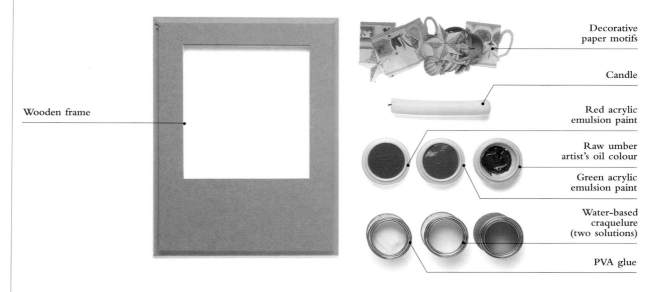

Wooden frame

Decorative paper motifs

Candle

Red acrylic emulsion paint

Raw umber artist's oil colour

Green acrylic emulsion paint

Water-based craquelure (two solutions)

PVA glue

1 *Rub sandpaper wrapped around a block over the surface of the wooden frame to smooth any rough edges and give the surface of the wood a slight key. Mix red acrylic emulsion paint with water until it is the consistency of single cream and apply a coat over the front of the frame. Allow to dry.*

2 *Rub a candle over the entire surface of the frame to coat it with a layer of wax. Then wipe off the excess flakes of wax.*

3 *Mix green acrylic emulsion paint with water to the consistency of single cream and apply a coat over the front of the frame. Allow to dry. Rub a pad of wire wool in a circular motion over the entire frame (see inset). This will remove some of the green paint and expose the layer of red paint underneath.*

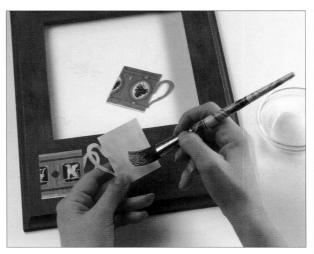

4 Select your motifs to decorate the frame. These can be colour-copied to the required size or used as they are. Paint a layer of dilute PVA glue over the motifs and allow to dry before cutting them out. This strengthens the paper and helps prevent tearing. Cut out the motifs using a scalpel and cutting mat for straight edges, and a pair of small nail scissors for fiddly curves.

5 Arrange the paper motifs on the frame until you are satisfied with the design. Brush the back of the motifs with dilute PVA glue and stick them in positon on the frame. Dab a scrunched-up paper towel over the motifs to smooth out air bubbles and absorb any excess glue. Ensure that all the edges are stuck down and leave to dry.

6 To create the antique look of cracked varnish, apply one coat of water-based craquelure over the frame and allow to dry. (Craquelure is usually sold in two solutions and it is advisable to follow the manufacturer's instructions.) Apply a second coat (for fine cracks) and allow to dry. Finally, apply a coat of the second solution. Allow to dry and colourless cracks will slowly form across the surface.

7 Using a soft cloth, rub a large blob of raw umber artist's oil colour into the cracks over the surface of the frame. Rub off the excess paint with the cloth and buff the frame to polish it. The dark colour will stay in the cracks to create an aged look.

Driftwood and Seashells

MATERIALS
Driftwood

Rope

Wood battening, 2 x 4cm (¾ x 1½in) thick

PVA glue

Nails (optional)

Glass

Mount

Hardboard, for backing

4 frame turns and screws

2 screws, 12mm (½in) long

Seashells

Seaweed

EQUIPMENT
Ruler

Saw

Clamp

Screwdriver

Craft knife

Cigarette lighter

BEACHCOMBING IS ONE of life's great pleasures, and nothing is such an effective antidote to trouble and stress as walking along the seashore, collecting shells and flotsam, and listening to the sound of the waves. The charm of these driftwood frames lies in their rugged, nautical texture, an appealingly countrified character, and muted colour which flatters all sorts of pictures from a moody sepia photograph to the most delicate watercolour painting.

Driftwood frames are the perfect choice for rural retreats and are a welcome recollection of wide open spaces for city dwellers. With their subtle understated appearance, they would fit in easily with natural colours and fabrics, as well as holding their own in more sophisticated interiors.

For the designer, the charm of driftwood frames lies in their spontaneity – no two pieces are ever the same. Their design has to be guided by the materials, a process requiring the same careful concentration as putting together a jigsaw puzzle. It is this feature that makes every driftwood frame unique.

Flattering Flotsam
The wider your choice of driftwood the better – smooth, rounded pieces, perhaps with remnants of paint, give a subtle finish; small, jagged, twiggy pieces are more rustic. The two can be combined, and any amount of seashells, pebbles or dried seaweed can adorn the frame. To complete the seaside theme, flaunt a little flotilla on the shelf beneath.

Shorelines
Winter, with a biting east wind and immediately after a violent storm, is the most fruitful time to pick among the pebbles for sea-treasures. The frame then becomes a souvenir along with the delicately evocative watercolour.

16

Making and Decorating the Frame

*A pleasure to put together from a seaside treasure
trove, this driftwood frame would be the perfect souvenir
of a summer idyll.*

Wood battening

Driftwood

Seashells
and seaweed

Nails

PVA glue

Rope

Mount

Hardboard
backing

Glass

Screws and frame turns

1 *Collect pieces of driftwood and rope from a beach.
Select pieces of a manageable size. Leave the driftwood
in a warm place like an airing cupboard or sunny window-
sill to dry. This may take a few days if the wood is damp.*

2 *Saw the wood battening into four pieces, two
measuring 20cm (8in) long, and two measuring 25cm
(10in) long. Using PVA glue, stick the pieces of battening
together to make a frame. Leave to dry in a clamp (see p.9)
for at least four hours. The corners of the frame can be
nailed for extra security, if preferred.*

3 *Using PVA glue, stick pieces of driftwood onto the frame, covering the front, outer sides, top and bottom of the frame. Choose interesting looking pieces of driftwood and allow it to overlap the edges of the frame. Don't worry if there are any gaps between the pieces – these can be filled later with shells or seaweed.*

4 *Lay the frame face down and, working from the back of the frame, glue several thinner pieces of driftwood to the inner sides of the frame, covering only half the width of the battening. These thin strips will form the rebate of the frame, to hold the picture and backing in place. Leave the frame to dry for approximately 24 hours.*

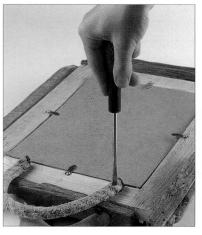

5 *Lay the frame face down, and carefully insert the glass, mount and picture, all cut to size, in the back of the frame. Check from the front of the frame that the picture is central within the frame and mount. Lay the hardboard backing on top of the picture and secure in place by screwing in one frame turn in the centre of each side of the frame.*

6 *Using a craft knife, trim the rope to a length of approximately 20cm (8in). This will form the hanging hook for the frame. Singe the ends of the rope with a cigarette lighter to prevent it unravelling. Then screw the ends of the rope to the back of the frame, positioning them above the hardboard backing and an equal distance from each side edge.*

7 *Turn the frame the right way up and fill in any gaps in the driftwood decoration by gluing in seashells and pieces of seaweed. Allow the frame to dry.*

Stars and Hearts

MATERIALS
Paper
Wooden frame
Acetate
Black, green and red acrylic emulsion paint
Gold powder
PVA glue
Water-based acrylic varnish

EQUIPMENT
Pencil
Ruler
Waterproof felt-tip pen
Scalpel
Paintbrush
Sponge
Hole punch
Small dish
Varnish brush

STENCILS ARE ALL THINGS to all people; in the days of flower power, when the word "natural" meant all was right with the world, stencilled roses erupted on walls, trailing honeysuckle wreathed wastepaper bins, bunches of grapes burst from innocent filing cabinets and morning glory twined about the toilet. One tended to feel akin to a browsing aphid among the greenery.

Stencils have since moved on, and, with a grateful nod to their traditions in 18th-century Britain and North America, they are flourishing as a convenient and easy method of repeating a design. Aesthetically, stencils capture a contemporary approach to decor, being both casual and precise. They lend themselves to subtle blends of colour and soft uneven paint techniques. Strong tonal contrasts have a naive charm, while stippled muted designs work well with faded tapestry. It is child's play to steal motifs from favourite fabrics in a discreet visual pun. Ethnic textiles can be echoed in colour and pattern to their mutual enrichment. The secret is to use broken colour – flat colour on a plain background looks too harsh.

Patchwork Granny
The strong plain colours and geometric shapes of Amish pieced quilts transfer well to stencils, and make a fitting surround to a revered ancestor who might well have done the odd bit of quilting herself. The Amish were particularly fond of using black – usually somewhat faded – as a foil to bright colour. Here the background is more of a dark earthy grey; pure black would be too extreme.

Three Easy Pieces
The only tricky aspect with stencils is getting a repeat pattern to "behave" at the corners. If your frame is square this simplifies matters, otherwise it is best to work from the corners and use a single central motif to fill gaps.

Decorating the Frame

Cutting tiny shapes is tricky; if you want a small motif as punctuation, you can raid your office for a hole punch to make miniature circles. Failing this, small squares or triangles are manageable with a scalpel.

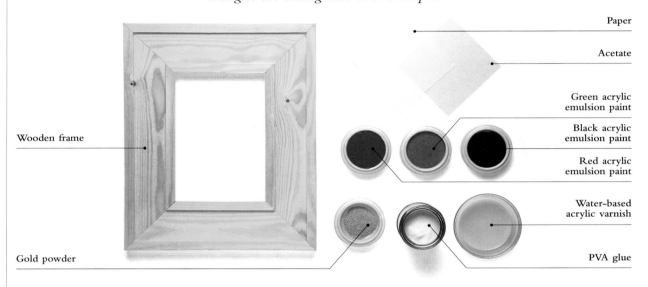

Paper

Acetate

Green acrylic emulsion paint

Black acrylic emulsion paint

Red acrylic emulsion paint

Water-based acrylic varnish

Wooden frame

Gold powder

PVA glue

1 *Using books or magazines as reference, sketch out a design for your frame. This symmetrical design comprises triangles and ovals, the sizes of which were worked out to fit the dimensions of the frame.*

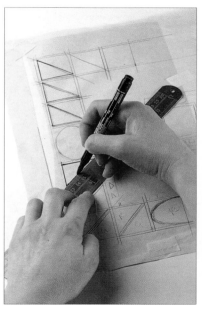

2 *Draw the design onto acetate using a waterproof felt-tip pen. Ensure that you leave enough "bridges" or strips of acetate between each shape. Cut out the shapes carefully with a scalpel.*

3 *Paint the frame, including inner and outer edges, with a coat of black acrylic emulsion. Leave to dry.*

4 *Position the acetate stencil on the frame and secure it in place. Dip a sponge in green acrylic emulsion, dab off the excess, then sponge over alternating triangles and the side ovals of the stencil. Don't worry if you dab some paint onto other areas of the frame – this can be touched up later.*

5 *Cut out another stencil for the alternating red triangles. Position the acetate over the frame, lining it up accurately. Sponge red acrylic emulsion over the remaining triangles and ovals. When dry, touch up the frame with black acrylic emulsion as necessary. Leave to dry.*

6 *Next make a stencil of a row of dots. A simple and effective way to do this is to use a hole punch, which saves laborious cutting with a scalpel.*

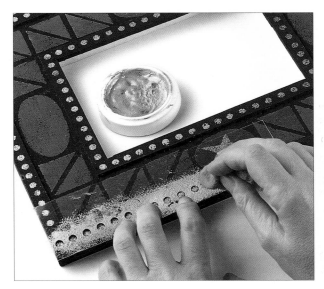

7 *Mix some gold powder with PVA glue in a small dish. Position the dot stencil on the inner edge of the frame and sponge gold lightly over the stencil. Repeat on the outer edge of the frame. Allow to dry.*

8 *Make star and heart stencils for the ovals of the frame. Position on the frame then sponge gold over each stencil in turn. When the frame is dry, apply a coat of varnish.*

Colourwashed Wood

MATERIALS

Length of wood, 5 x
2.5cm (2 x 1in) thick
PVA glue
Wood filler (optional)
Beeswax furniture
polish or
petroleum jelly
Acrylic paints
Mirror, 44cm
(17½in) square
Cardboard, 44cm
(17½in) square
4 mirror corners
Brown gummed tape
2 mirror plates
Screws

EQUIPMENT

Ruler
Saw
Housepainter's brush
Coarse-grade
sandpaper
Screwdriver

THE VICTORIANS had a curious and misplaced passion for woodgraining – it is hard to see why one should labour to simulate perfect grain patterns when one can so easily enjoy the natural look of wood as it comes, with all its knots and irregularities. The natural woodgrain on this frame has been accentuated using layered transparent tones of blue-green paint, while the knots in the wood have been picked out with beeswax as a resist. It would be a challenge to find anything simpler than these four pieces of wood to make a frame, but the result has a quiet sophistication that requires nothing more.

Try using different dilutions of water-based paint in toning or wildly contrasting colours, or use colour over a base of wood stain, dye or even ink for further variation. With a technique of such simplicity, using such easily available materials, you can feel free to try out whatever idea comes to mind.

The casual exploitation of the intrinsic texture and qualities of wood is accentuated here by the use of antiqued silver leaf mirror glass. You can buy this in various finishes or the brave can experiment and make it themselves.

Romantic Reflections
The irregular silver-leafed mirror in this frame gives a gloriously soft-focus reflection, and has an intriguing texture that makes plain mirror glass look unutterably dull in comparison. Lilies and a blackened silver candelabra emphasize the elegance of this simple frame.

Muted Pewter Colours
Softer and quieter colours are wonderfully effective in summoning up a look of times long past. It may seem obvious, but there is nothing to stop you hanging your mirror vertically or horizontally as best fits the space you have.

Making and Decorating the Frame

*This wooden frame, which is as simple as
can be, exploits the natural pattern and texture of
humble pine planks.*

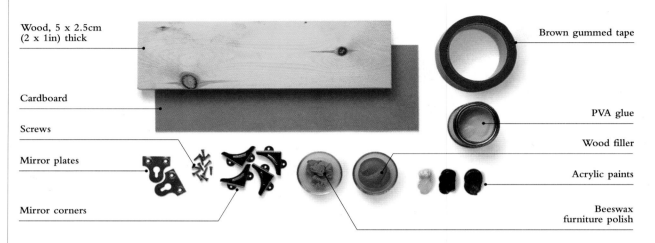

Wood, 5 x 2.5cm
(2 x 1in) thick

Cardboard

Screws

Mirror plates

Mirror corners

Brown gummed tape

PVA glue

Wood filler

Acrylic paints

Beeswax
furniture polish

1 *Saw the length of wood into four pieces, two measuring 42.5cm (17in) long, and two measuring 35cm (14in) long. Assemble the frame by gluing the four pieces of wood together using PVA glue. Leave to dry overnight with weights on top.*

2 *Fill the corner joins of the frame with wood filler if necessary. Rub the frame down thoroughly with coarse-grade sandpaper to remove any rough edges and unevenness in the wood. Using your finger, apply small blobs of beeswax furniture polish or petroleum jelly on any knots in the wood and rub in with your finger to spread the wax on the surface. Leave the frame to dry overnight.*

3 *Apply a coat of blue-green acrylic paint diluted 1:3 with water over the front of the frame. Where the wax has been applied, the paint will be resisted. Allow the paint to dry, then turn the frame over and paint a 12mm (½in) blue-green border around the inner edge of the frame (see inset). This is to prevent the pale colour of the wood being reflected when the mirror is inserted into the frame.*

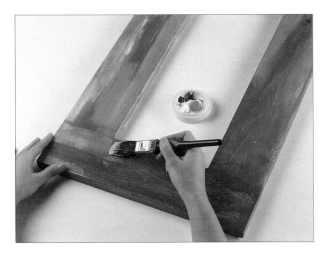

4 *When the first coat of paint is dry, roughly brush on a coat of lighter blue-green paint, together with some streaks of white, and leave to dry again.*

5 *Rub sandpaper over the entire frame to expose some of the layers of paint and create a distressed effect. Rub the sandpaper more vigorously over the knottier parts of the wood so that these become more apparent.*

6 *To soften the distressed effect, cover the whole frame with a wash of the original blue-green acrylic paint, this time diluted 1:4 with water.*

7 *When the paint is completely dry, turn the frame over and position the mirror over the central hole. Place the cardboard on top of the mirror and secure in place with a mirror corner screwed to each corner. Tape the edges of the cardboard down with brown gummed tape. Finally, screw one mirror plate to each side, approximately 19cm (7½in) from the top of the frame.*

Jewelled Silver Frame

MATERIALS

Thick cardboard
Double-sided sticky tape
Picture
Acetate
Tin foil
Flat-backed glass droplets
Glass beads
String
Superglue

EQUIPMENT

Pencil
Metal ruler
Scalpel
Biro
Scissors
Bradawl

MAKING THIS jokey extrovert frame – with a supervising adult to wield scalpel, superglue and bradawl – is just the thing to keep fractious children quietly occupied on a rainy afternoon. The materials are cheap and easy to come by, and the technique lends itself as much to wiggly infant scribbles as to fastidious Celtic curlicues drawn by an expert hand.

This particular frame is tiny, just large enough to accommodate a shocking pink valentine. The big frosted beads and glowing spheres of molten glass give this little frame a dash of colour, and refine the silver and glass in cheeky contrast to the hank of coarse twine from which it hangs. You could use the same method to make a more generous-sized frame, or you could change the shape to a heart, diamond, circle or whatever you fancy. If you make the "window" any shape other than square or rectangular, you will have to use an extra strip of foil to cover the cardboard which will show through.

Completely Foiled
There is nothing pretentious about this little picture frame. Quickly and easily put together, it is cheerfully reminiscent of the punched and embossed tinware from Central America, and works well with bright colours and ethnic textiles.

Hearts on Show
These two, slightly more dignified, frames were made using heavier aluminium foil, which is harder to come by and use but has greater resilience. The pendant heart was made by wrapping foil around a cardboard shape.

Making and Decorating the Frame
*Quick, easy and fun to make, this frame is the perfect
sparkly setting for favourite memorabilia.*

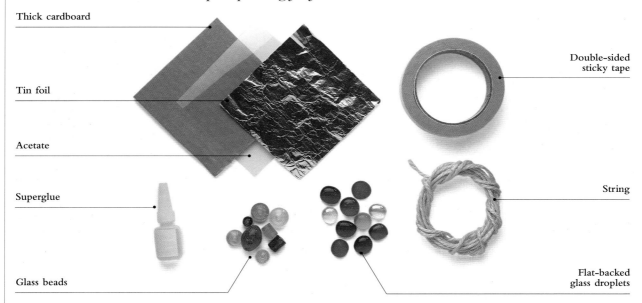

Thick cardboard

Tin foil

Acetate

Superglue

Glass beads

Double-sided
sticky tape

String

Flat-backed
glass droplets

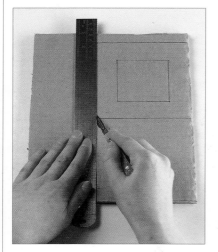

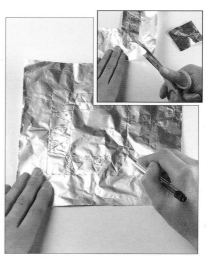

1 *Draw two squares on a piece of
cardboard and cut them out using
a metal ruler and scalpel. Cut out
and discard a smaller square from the
centre of one to form the aperture of
the frame. This cardboard square will
be the top square of the frame.*

2 *Using double-sided sticky tape,
stick a picture in the middle of the
bottom cardboard square. Then stick a
piece of acetate, 12mm (½in) smaller
all around than the cardboard square,
over the top of the picture.*

3 *Using the scissors, cut out a
square of tin foil 5cm (2in) larger
on each side than the cardboard
squares. Using a biro, draw shapes on
the foil within the frame area to create
a raised pattern on the reverse side.
Cut out the central aperture 3mm
(⅛in) smaller on each side than the
aperture in the top square of
cardboard. Make a diagonal cut in
each corner (see inset).*

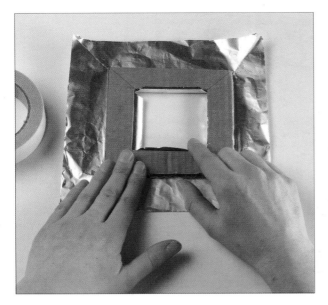

4 *Using double-sided sticky tape, attach the top piece of cardboard to the foil, positioning the apertures so that they match exactly. Fold the inner edges of the foil into the aperture in the top piece of cardboard.*

5 *Attach the bottom piece of cardboard, with the picture facing downwards, over the top piece, using double-sided sticky tape. Stick pieces of tape around the edges of the foil, and then fold these outer edges back over the cardboard frame to secure, tucking in the corners neatly.*

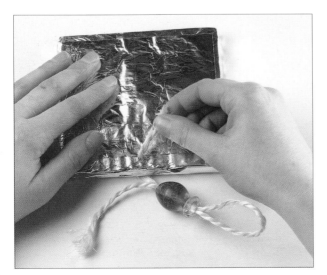

6 *Turn the frame the right way up and, using a bradawl, carefully pierce a hole through the top of the frame, from front to back. Make a hanging loop by threading two glass beads onto a loop of string. Thread one end of the string through the pierced hole in the frame from front to back. Knot the ends together and secure with superglue.*

7 *To complete the frame decoration, stick brightly coloured glass droplets to each corner on the front of the frame with superglue. Leave to dry.*

Touches of Gold

MATERIALS

Wooden moulding
PVA glue
Wood filler
Black wood stain
Mount board
Oil-based gold paint
White acrylic paint
Cardboard
Backing card
Nails
Brown gummed tape
2 hooks and cord

EQUIPMENT

Mitring block
Tenon saw
Clamp
Sandpaper
Housepainter's brush
Scalpel
Pencil
Artist's brush
Stippling brush
Wire wool
Cloth

THIS ELEGANTLY UNDERSTATED FRAME is the perfect starting point for frame-making and the method can be used to produce something as grand or as folksy as you want. If you have ever been mesmerized by all the different kinds of coving and beading sold in timber merchants, and longed for some way of exploiting this treasure trove, your problem is solved. All you need is a pot of glue and a few short lengths for experimentation, and you can produce multiple variations using different mouldings and wood stain. Accuracy in cutting and mitring the timber is important. If you can use the specific equipment for frame-making you will not need recourse to such quantities of wood filler and your finished frame will have a look of professional smoothness.

Experiment with combinations of different wood dyes and acrylic top-coats to achieve subtle veils of colour that will co-ordinate with your decor and any print you may have a mind to use. Here the delicate striations and moiré effect of the wood showing through the colour give a surface richness that is satisfying without being overwhelming.

Candlelit Classic
The warm flickering light of candles is just the thing to bring the medallions and flakes of gold to life on this simple frame, and to show up the lively pattern of the wood.

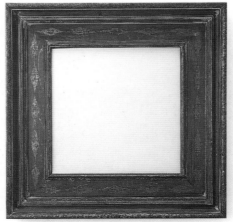

Variations on a Theme of Wood
The same all-purpose frame-making technique can be employed with subtle variations of colour and differing proportions to make a satisfying group.

Making and Decorating the Frame

*Simple to make and darkly effective, the mysterious glitter
and stipple of this frame would adapt well to different
mouldings and colours.*

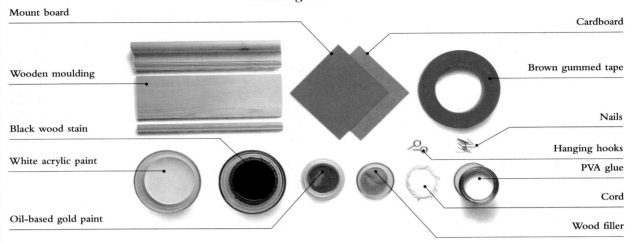

Mount board

Wooden moulding

Black wood stain

White acrylic paint

Oil-based gold paint

Cardboard

Brown gummed tape

Nails

Hanging hooks

PVA glue

Cord

Wood filler

1 *Make a basic frame from wooden moulding (see pp. 8–9). Build up this basic frame by gluing on a wider outer frame and a narrower inner frame, using different mouldings, to create a three-layered frame. Leave in a clamp to dry overnight (see p. 9).*

2 *Fill in any holes in the joins with wood filler, then rub the frame with sandpaper to smooth down rough edges. Paint a layer of black wood stain over the frame using bold sweeping strokes to cover the area quickly.*

3 Make a simple stencil by cutting out a circle from a piece of mount board using a scalpel. The circle should be small enough to fit the width of the frame. Use the stencil to draw a circle at intervals around the frame, pressing hard with your pencil to make grooves in the wood.

4 Using an artist's brush, carefully fill in the pencilled circles with gold paint. The paint will collect in the pencilled grooves, adding to the decorative effect of the stencilled pattern.

5 Dip a stippling brush or sponge in the gold paint, dab the excess paint off on a piece of cardboard, then dab the brush randomly over the frame for a decorative broken pattern. Leave the frame to dry.

6 To soften the black and gold colouring, apply a coat of white acrylic paint over the front of the frame and leave to dry.

7 Rub the paint back using wire wool. Then buff the frame with a soft cloth to bring up the gold. Insert the mount, picture and backing card in the back of the frame, securing with nails and brown gummed tape (see p.9). Attach hanging hooks and cord to the back of the frame to finish (see p.9).

Glittering Trail

MATERIALS

MDF board, 6mm
(¼in) thick, for base
MDF board, 16mm
(⅝in) thick, for sides
PVA glue
Mirror
Water
Silver smalti
Vitreous glass tesserae
Tile grout
Mirror plates
and screws

EQUIPMENT

Ruler
Tenon saw
Housepainter's brush
Clamps
Felt-tip pen
Scalpel
Safety goggles
Mosaic nippers
Rubber gloves
Squeegee
Cloth
Bowl
Screwdriver

MOSAIC IS A MYSTERY until you realize that the tesserae, mirror or ceramic pieces are glued first, and then the filler is smoothed over the top. This is a naughty modern invention, far quicker and more manageable than the traditional direct method (where the tesserae are individually embedded in mortar) or indirect method (where the tesserae are stuck face-down to strong paper and then bedded in mortar in panels).

Having grasped this basic principle of mosaic, you may wish to plunder the Roman repertoire of geometric borders and strong, vigorous designs for replication on your frames. The Romans had a thoroughly impressionist way with colour, and a cheerful opportunism when it came to materials. Faceted glass jewels, amethyst quartz and mother-of-pearl discs sit quite happily with coloured and gold glass squares (smalti to you and me). For a more contemporary source of inspiration you could take a trip to Barcelona to study the astounding work of Antonio Gaudí at first hand. Here, at last, is a use for those heart-breaking accidents with the washing up.

Snail's Pace

For those who do not spring energetically to life in the morning, the contemplation of a meandering snail, leaving a glittering silver trail, may bring comfort to those early ablutions. A mutable spectrum of different greens makes a congenial background; the more variations of a single colour you can lay hands on, the livelier the finished effect will be.

Gastropod at Large
With the dogged persistence typical of snails, this specimen has escaped its boundaries and is making for the open spaces. This snail has been hand-painted on a tile, using the raku technique.

36

Making and Decorating the Frame

*Using this unorthodox method, assembling the piece into a
design is quick and easy. As you gain confidence, you
might wish to experiment with pebbles, shells, glass gems
or prized pieces of broken china.*

MDF board for sides

PVA glue

Mirror

Vitreous glass tesserae

MDF board for base

Silver smalti

Vitreous glass tesserae

Tile grout

Mirror plates and screws

1 *Build a simple frame from
medium density fibreboard
(MDF). Cut out a rectangular base
using a tenon saw; saw four side
pieces to fit. Using PVA glue, stick
two side pieces on the base to make a
right-angled corner. Glue the mirror to
the base, butting it up to the corner,
then glue on the remaining two sides.
Clamp and leave it to dry overnight.*

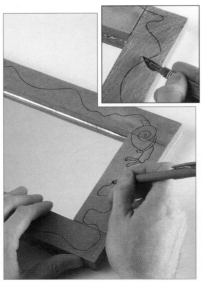

2 *Seal the frame with a mix of 1
part PVA to 1 part water; allow
to dry. Draw a design on the frame
with a felt-tip pen. Here the artist has
designed a snail with its trail going
around the frame. Choose a design
that has good colour contrast. Score
the frame with a scalpel or sharp knife
(see inset) to create a key to the
surface. This helps the mosaic adhere.*

3 *Using mosaic nippers, cut the
silver smalti into small pieces.
These will be used for the snail trail.
Always wear safety goggles when
using mosaic nippers, as pieces of
smalti can fly everywhere.*

4 *Apply a bead of PVA glue along the marked snail trail. Lay pieces of smalti along the glue, butting up the pieces to each other. Use the mosaic nippers to "nibble" the smalti, cutting it up into smaller shapes as desired.*

5 *Make the snail using a mixture of yellow, orange and brown tesserae. To build up the pattern, start at the centre of the snail shell and spiral outwards. Finish with the snail's head and antennae.*

6 *Apply PVA glue along the inner rim of the frame, then stick down green-coloured tesserae so that they jut up slightly over the edge. This will allow the tesserae that is to be applied on top of the frame to butt up against them, thus making a neat edge.*

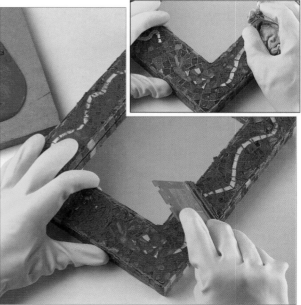

7 *Apply tesserae to the outer edge of the frame in the same way. Then build up the green patterning on the top of the frame, following the curve of the snail trail to create movement and flow. Use the mosaic nippers to shape the tesserae as you require.*

8 *Leave the completed mosaic to dry for a day. Mix tile grout to mud-pie consistency, or use ready-made grout. Wearing rubber gloves and using a flexible squeegee, apply grout generously over the frame. Clean the grout off the frame using a cloth dipped in cold water and wrung out (see inset). The grout will remain in the areas between the tesserae – the interstices. Leave to dry, then attach mirror plates on the back (see p.9).*

Rustic Chicken Frame

MATERIALS

Tracing paper
Driftwood, 25mm
(1in thick)
Plywood, 9mm
(⅜in) thick
Wood glue
Tacks
Oil paints
Turpentine
Copper
Nails
Thin wire
Mirror
Cardboard
2 mirror plates
and screws

EQUIPMENT

Pencil
Coping saw
Hammer
Housepainter's brush
Artist's brush
Tin snips
Piercing saw
Pliers
Screwdriver

THERE IS NO REASON why frames need to be serious. This pair of hens has a wayward sense of humour that will appeal to all but the most earnest. The frame is carefully constructed so that the frisky chicken candleholders can slide from side to side, though, somewhat perversely, they are positioned so that it is impossible to reflect their candle-light in the glass. However, you could lengthen the slots in the base of the frame if you passionately wished to use the sconce in the traditional way – to maximize candle-power.

Despite its insouciant air, this is a fairly difficult frame to make, and accuracy is essential in the cutting and assembly of wood and copper. However, the reward is a witty mirror frame with a weather-worn, countrified look, which will always make you feel like whistling something from *Oklahoma*! If these ornery old speckled hens do not appeal, you might research the charms of the dapper Scots Dumpy, the elegant Silver Spangles or the rich russet of the familiar Rhode Island Red. A visit to a farm museum will reveal that there is a lot more to chickens than simply beak and wattles.

A Tale of Two Chickens
Beak to beak, wattles rampant, these two bucolic birds double as doughty candle-bearers on this witty mirror frame.

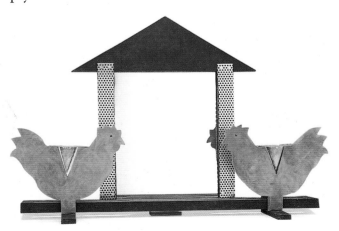

Metallic Mirror
For a more high-tech variation, the clucking confrontation takes place in front of a nifty neo-Palladian mirror embellished with punctured metal pilasters.

Making and Decorating the Frame

Textured driftwood and plywood chickens are used in this whimsical mirror sconce, which, despite its carefree air, is one of the more complicated frames to tackle. Ensure that the wood is cut accurately so that all the elements of the frame can slot together smoothly.

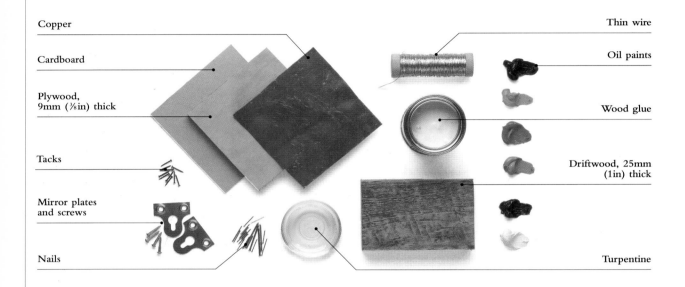

Copper

Cardboard

Plywood, 9mm (⅜in) thick

Tacks

Mirror plates and screws

Nails

Thin wire

Oil paints

Wood glue

Driftwood, 25mm (1in) thick

Turpentine

1 *Photocopy the templates for the frame (see p.90) to the required size. Trace templates A to C onto driftwood and templates D to G onto plywood and cut them out with a coping saw. You should have a total of 12 pieces.*

2 *Using wood glue, stick the two uprights (C) into the slots in the base of the frame (B). Glue the roof (A) to the top of the uprights, ensuring they are level.*

3 *Make the runners for the chickens. Glue and then tack piece G to piece F to make an L-shape. Glue and then tack the chicken to piece F so that it is 3cm (1½in) away from piece G. Repeat to make the second runner.*

4 *Insert the runner into the base of the frame so that piece G protrudes through the slot. Glue and tack piece E to the top of piece G and the side of the chicken to secure the runner in place. Repeat to attach the second runner to the base.*

5 *Paint the frame base, uprights and roof, both front and back, with blue oil paint diluted to the ratio of 1:20 with turpentine and leave to dry. Paint the chickens with diluted orange oil paint and again leave to dry before painting further.*

6 *Using an artist's brush, stipple a mix of orange, cadmium red, yellow ochre, lemon yellow and white oil paint over both chickens. Paint details such as eyes and beak on the chickens' heads.*

7 *For each candleholder, photocopy the templates H and I (see p.90) to the required size and trace onto copper. Using tin snips and a piercing saw, cut out each shape. Make holes as marked with a nail and hammer. Bend piece H to make a cone and place it on piece I. Loop thin wire through the holes to secure (see inset).*

8 *Turn the candleholders the right way up and nail them in place on the chickens. Insert the mirror in the back of the frame, add the cardboard backing cut slightly larger than the mirror, and secure in place with nails (see p.9). Attach mirror plates to the back of the mirror to finish (see p.9).*

Baronial Candle Sconce

MATERIALS

Thin steel
Candle
Mirror
Beeswax furniture
polish
Grate blackener

EQUIPMENT

Tracing paper
Pencil
Tin snips
File
Fine-grade wet and
dry paper
Block of wood
Hammer
Centre punch
Spot welder
Straight-edged pliers
Round-nosed pliers
Cloth
Wire wool

NOT EVERYONE has a spot welder lurking in the bottom of a cupboard. On the other hand, if you do happen to acquire one, you will be able to effect miracle cures for junk shop booty, such as broken tin trunks and interesting antique hat boxes with torn hinges, as well as making the odd baronial frame or two.

Metal frightens people quite unnecessarily – once you get the hang of it, and learn how to use it safely, you will find it no more problematical than cardboard and a good deal more malleable and handsome. Nothing beats glinting dark metal for drama, and it is a wonderful material to explore. You can cut it, mould it, shape it, give it texture, puncture it, and it will remain obediently as you want. Then you can blacken it, polish it or simply leave it plain.

If you are nervous of committing yourself to sheets of steel and equipment, you could begin your experiment with just a pair of tin snips and a couple of cans. Try embellishing a plain wooden frame with a few pieces of tin laid flat and nailed to the frame. Carefully done, this is a thrifty piece of recycling that looks surprisingly good.

Deceptively Butch
This frame would look just right in the echoing hallway of your Gothic pile, were it not for its diminutive size – it is only 18cm (7½in) by 11cm (4¾in). Tiny and perfectly formed, it is the ideal excuse to have a go at simple metalwork.

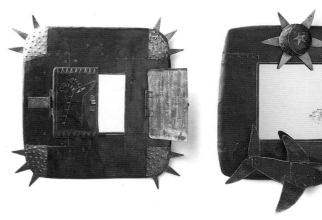

Sun, Moon and Dolphins
This eager dolphin will forever be bouncing through the waves under a composite celestial emblem. And for those who believe that mirrors should be hidden, you can put doors and spikes on a little mirror, as a reminder of the perils of vanity.

Making and Decorating the Frame

This hammered and textured dark metal frame, with a flickering candle flame reflected in its mirror glass, could bring a sense of drama as well as a touch of the castle to your home.

Thin steel

Beeswax furniture polish

Grate blackener

Candle

1 *Photocopy the templates for the frame (see p.91) to the required size, and trace them onto a piece of thin steel. Cut out all the components using tin snips. File all the edges straight, then rub with fine-grade wet and dry paper.*

2 *Place a corner piece (C) onto a block of wood, and punch a pattern of studs into it by hammering a centre punch into the metal at regular intervals. Repeat with the three remaining corner pieces.*

3 *Weld the four side pieces (A and B) together at the corners to form the basic frame. Weld the corner pieces onto the frame with the studs protruding upwards (see inset).*

4 *Weld the five spikes (E) onto the semi-circle (D), ensuring that they are spaced evenly. This will form the base of the candleholder at the front of the mirror frame.*

5 *Using straight-edged pliers, bend the small strip for the candleholder (F) at a right angle. Then bend it around a candle using round-nosed pliers. This forms the top part of the candleholder. Ensure there is at least a 3mm (⅛in) "stem" to hold the candle away from the mirror. With the round-nosed pliers, curl the spikes of the candleholder base downwards. Weld the candleholder pieces onto the centre base of the frame (see inset).*

6 *Using straight-edged pliers, carefully bend the four mirror backing corners (G) into shape. These will hold the mirror in place on the back of the frame.*

7 *Place the mirror face down on the back of the frame, ensuring there is a 12mm (½in) overlap all the way around, and weld the mirror plates in position to secure the corners. Then bend piece (H) into the shape of a hanging hook and weld it in place at the top centre of the back of the frame.*

8 *Rub a soft cloth dipped in a little beeswax furniture polish over the sides of the finished mirror frame, but not the corners, to bring out the shine. Buff up with a soft cloth.*

9 *Still using a soft cloth, rub grate blackener onto the frame corners. Then buff the corners with wire wool and fine-grade wet and dry paper to highlight the decorative effect of the pattern of raised studs.*

Ideas to Inspire

Wood and metal frames provide a starting point for a wealth of decorative effects in frame-making. As the frames in this section demonstrate, you can make a frame from any type of wood and leave it untreated, decorate it with paints or mosaic, or cover it with shells, baubles, tin cans, copper foil, string, cinnamon sticks, metal studs, or anything else you might fancy. Above all, experiment and have fun!

▼ Tiny Box Frame
This simply constructed box frame, measuring 12.5cm (5in) square, is decorated with a combination of pencils, crayons, pens and paints, to make a perfect match with the ceramic figure set inside.

▲ Wood on Wood
Made from driftwood, this frame relies on textural contrast for impact, juxtaposing sea-battered driftwood with a smooth, sanded wooden base. The carved wooden avocet is secured to the frame by delicate metal legs.

▶ Paint and Pigment
Constructed simply from pieces of old wood, this frame is painted to echo the colours of the Mexican doll collage, then rubbed with gold pigment and sealed with varnish.

◀ Lettered Frame
A simple wooden box frame is transformed with a coat of acrylic gesso and a wash of acrylic paint, then decorated with lettering and drawing pencil.

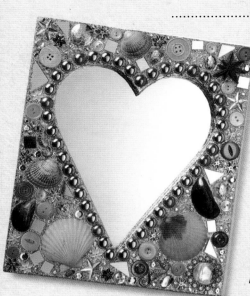

◀ Kitsch Delight
Starting with a chipboard base, this mirror frame is first covered with crumpled gold foil, then decorated with a magpie motley of shells, buttons, sequins and pieces of glass. Gold furnishing studs surround the heart-shaped mirror.

▶ Colourful Arch
This arched mirror frame is decorated with pieces of broken china, in a range of greens, blues and purples, held together with blue-coloured grout.

▶ Clean and Simple
This tactile box frame is constructed entirely from driftwood and has received no treatment other than a thorough sanding by hand to achieve its ultra-smooth finish, in perfect partnership with the minimalist painting within. Its clean, simple lines convey a great sense of balance.

▼ Adrift at Sea

A single piece of driftwood, with characteristic peeling paint and rough-textured edges, has been cut to make this simple yet effective frame, used to display a nautical needlepoint picture.

▶ Wired Sunburst

A dainty sunburst of six wire rays soldered to a wire circle. Added decoration comes in the form of a glass blob suspended by finer wire in the centre of each ray.

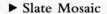

▶ Slate Mosaic

This chunky mosaic frame is made from an assortment of smalti, vitreous glass, broken plates and tiles, and slabs of slate. They are attached to a wooden frame using tile adhesive for the ceramic pieces and silicone adhesive for the slate.

◄ Fishy Frame
First stained with watercolour paint, this wooden frame was then decorated with PVA stars and swirls, pieces of foil, sweet papers, cellophane and sequins, before being further embellished with acrylics and gold paint.

► Valentine Mirror
This folksy frame made from hand-painted MDF (medium density fibreboard) decorated with colourful fabric hearts and circles would make the perfect Valentine's Day gift.

▼ Beaten Metal Frame
This unusual homage to scrap was made by nailing beaten sections of tin cans around a wooden frame. The tin was then burnt with a blow lamp to achieve an aged patina.

▲ Stencilled Drama
Simple to do, this frame achieves great dramatic impact with its use of different paint textures and strange bird-like stencilled motifs set against its dark background.

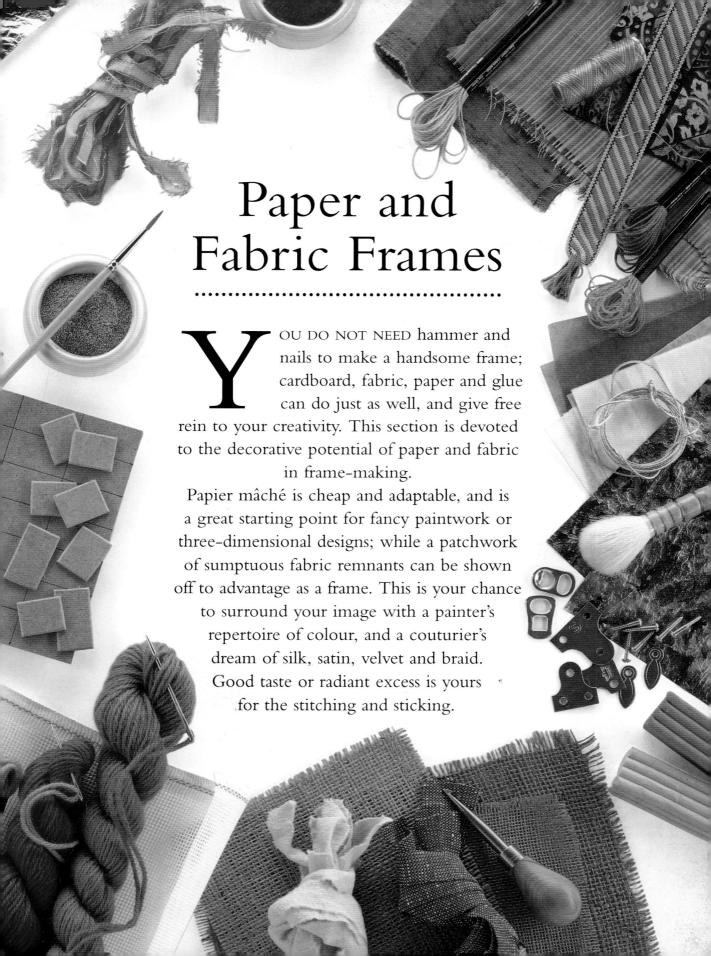

Paper and Fabric Frames

··

YOU DO NOT NEED hammer and nails to make a handsome frame; cardboard, fabric, paper and glue can do just as well, and give free rein to your creativity. This section is devoted to the decorative potential of paper and fabric in frame-making.

Papier mâché is cheap and adaptable, and is a great starting point for fancy paintwork or three-dimensional designs; while a patchwork of sumptuous fabric remnants can be shown off to advantage as a frame. This is your chance to surround your image with a painter's repertoire of colour, and a couturier's dream of silk, satin, velvet and braid. Good taste or radiant excess is yours for the stitching and sticking.

Fishes and Squiggles

MATERIALS

Plywood, 12mm
(½in) thick
Plywood, 6mm
(¼in) thick
PVA glue
Tacks
Paper
Water
Matt oil-based paint
Silver metal transfer
Decorator's acrylic
gloss varnish
Mirror
Cardboard
Nails
Brown gummed tape
2 D-ring hangers

EQUIPMENT

Pencil
Ruler
Coping saw
Sandpaper
Hammer
Scissors
Large bowl
Blender
Spatula (optional)
Housepainter's brush
Varnish brush
Screwdriver

PAPIER MACHE is a wonderfully simple way to give character to plain plywood and to add three-dimensional motifs to a flat surface. Paper pulp, which can be moulded to any shape, has been used on this frame to create fish and squiggles for a frisky seaside flavour. You could make a mirror with hearts and arrows for the love of your life, or astrological signs combined with sun, stars and moons for anyone with a taste for the occult. Whatever design you choose, remember to keep it simple – the effect of the hand-moulded shapes picked out with silver metal transfer is bold and dramatic, and attempting something much more complex will lessen the impact, as well as drive you to extremes of vexation.

This is an exuberant sculptural frame, and not the best one to tackle if you don't like to get your hands sticky. There is no alternative to mixing the paper pulp and glue by hand, and the smoothing and shaping of the surface is best achieved with slightly dampened fingers. On the other hand, squelching paper pulp between the fingers can bring back fond memories of infancy, and making the pulp is as soothing as kneading dough.

Perfect for Pisceans
A cool and uncluttered mirror frame, perfectly at home in a cool and uncluttered bathroom – a banal but important piece of advice is to seal it thoroughly against steam or accidental dowsing in the wash-basin. This frame would make a perfect gift for any Pisceans among your acquaintances.

Mayan Motifs
These simple shapes, probably based on some prehistoric archaeological find, have a pleasant irregularity and suggest the hand of the maker. In an age of standardized mass-production, such touches of personality are something to be prized.

Making and Decorating the Frame

*Vibrant turquoise, decorated with silver hieroglyphics
and fish, combine to make a frame with an air of
Mexican panache.*

Thick plywood

Thin plywood

Cardboard

Brown
gummed tape

Decorator's
acrylic gloss
varnish

PVA glue

Matt oil-
based paint

Silver metal
transfer

Tacks and nails

D-ring hanger

Shredded paper

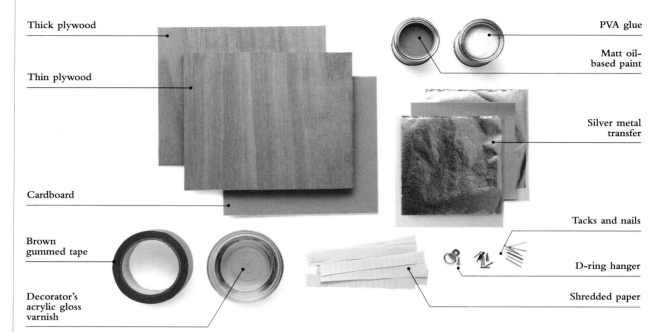

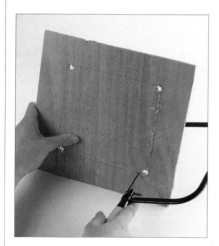

1 *Using a pencil and ruler, draw a square on thick plywood. Cut it out using a coping saw. Cut out a square in the centre. Sand the edges. Cut out a square of thinner plywood 5cm (2in) larger than the square aperture in the first piece. Cut out a square in this piece 2cm (¾in) smaller than the first aperture.*

2 *Using PVA glue, stick the smaller plywood square over the centre of the larger one – there should be a 1cm (½in) overlap around the inner edges of the frame. This is the rebate to hold the mirror. For extra security, tack the smaller plywood square to the larger one using at least three tacks on each side. Allow to dry.*

3 *To make the pulp, cut paper into strips and soak it overnight in water. Boil the soaked paper and water for 20 minutes, then liquidize in a blender and squeeze until dry. Add PVA glue in the proportion of 2 cups of PVA to 1 large bowl of pulp. Mix in well with your fingers to make the pulp smooth (see inset).*

4 *Lay the frame with the double side facing upwards, and spread a thin layer of PVA glue over the surface. Next cover the whole surface with paper pulp, smoothing it down with your hands or a spatula. Allow to dry for 48 hours until the papier mâché is firm to the touch.*

5 *To decorate the pulp base, first spread a thin layer of PVA glue over the area to be decorated, then add shapes made from wet pulp – here fish and squiggles – moulding and smoothing them in position with your fingers. Leave the frame to dry completely for 48 hours.*

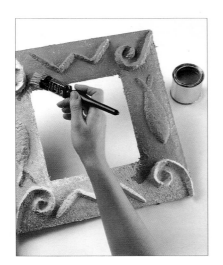

6 *Paint the entire frame, front and back, with a coat of turquoise paint. Allow the paint to dry for at least two hours.*

7 *Apply the silver metal transfer to the relief patterns. To do this, spread PVA glue over the relief areas, then cut the silver metal transfer to size and carefully press it over the relief areas, gently smoothing down with your finger. When dry, coat the silver decoration with a layer of acrylic gloss varnish.*

8 *When the varnish has dried, insert a mirror cut to size in the back of the frame. Lay the cardboard backing on top and nail in place (see p.9) to secure. Stick brown gummed tape over the cardboard edges to secure further and keep out dust and moisture. Finally screw in a D-ring hanger on each side of the back of the frame.*

Folk Stitches

MATERIALS

Paterna tapestry wool:
2 skeins cream (262),
1 skein red (842),
4 skeins blue (583)
12-mesh interlock
canvas, 29 x 33cm
(11½ x 13in)
Thick cardboard
Masking tape
Thin cardboard

EQUIPMENT

Tapestry needle
Scissors
Cloth
Steam iron
Pencil
Scalpel
Metal ruler
Pegs

NEEDLEPOINT IS the fashionable pastime for the glitterati of stage, screen and magazine; its quiet rhythm calms and soothes stressed nerves while waiting for the next moment of glory.

The neat geometric designs suggested by the grid structure of interlock canvas adapt surprisingly well to frames. If you are so inclined, you could probably be very ingenious with computer-aided design and create something personal using your initials combined with a Japanese kimono motif. Failing that, you could raid your childrens' schoolbooks for a few sheets of squared paper, and pass many happy hours trying out patterns with coloured crayons until you achieve a design you like. Old patchwork is a good source of ideas; stripes, checks, shadowed diamonds or cubes will all sit well around a frame.

For colours, you are spoiled for choice. Visit any haberdashery shop and you will find walls composed of hanks of tapestry wool in the most fastidious gradations of shade and tone. If colour excites you, choosing from this heady spectrum is a serious thrill.

Peasant Memories
A piece of pure nostalgia, the likes of this stylish French lady are highly unlikely to be seen today browsing in the Rue de Rivoli. The simple design of this needlepoint frame, reminiscent of the cross stitch beloved by country people all over Europe, has a decided affinity with her complicated embroidered garb.

Tricolour Encore
The same three colours look totally different when their emphasis is altered. The same design with red predominating is altogether sharper, and the complex design on the square frame has a more delicate impact.

Making the Frame

*Most people stitch in a definite direction, and usually end
up with more of a rhomboid than a rectangle. The answer
is to pull your tapestry into shape and steam iron it.*

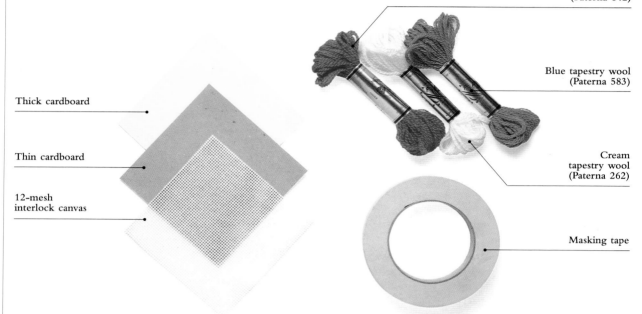

Red tapestry wool
(Paterna 842)

Blue tapestry wool
(Paterna 583)

Cream
tapestry wool
(Paterna 262)

Thick cardboard

Thin cardboard

12-mesh
interlock canvas

Masking tape

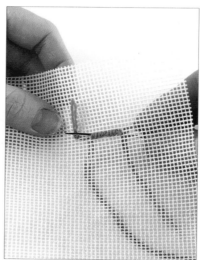

1 *Split the tapestry wool into
separate strands and thread the
needle with two strands. Make a knot
at one end. Starting in the top right
corner of the canvas, about 6cm (2½in)
in from the edge, insert the needle into
the canvas from above and bring it up
2cm (¾in) to the right.*

2 *Work tent stitch by inserting the
needle in the lower diagonal
square to the left of where the needle
came up. Bring the needle up in the
square directly above. Repeat, working
from right to left. When you reach the
knot, cut it off as you will have
secured the wool with your stitches.*

3 *When you reach the end of the
first row, work the next row from
left to right, and so on. The needle
will point alternately upwards and
downwards with each new row.
Follow the chart on p.91 when
stitching. Each square on the chart
represents one stitch on the canvas.*

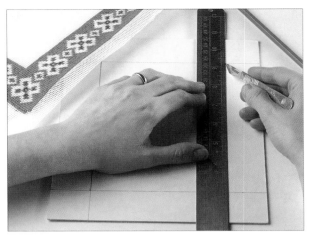

4 To change wool colour, simply take the needle to the back of the canvas, weave it through a few stitches then cut off the end. Start with a different colour as before and begin with a knot 2cm (¾in) to the left of where you want to begin stitching. Follow the chart to complete the stitching.

5 Trim the edges of the canvas. Press and shape your finished needlepoint with a cloth and steam iron. Draw the dimensions of the needlepoint on thick cardboard, making the finished size two stitch rows smaller all around the edge, to allow for the needlepoint to overlap the cardboard when assembling the frame. Using a scalpel and metal ruler, cut out the cardboard frame.

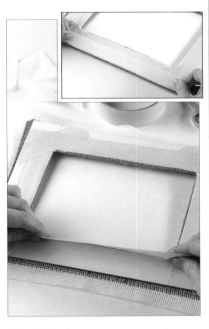

6 Cut out the frame aperture in the canvas using sharp scissors. Start at the centre and cut out to each corner so that you have four triangular flaps.

7 Place the needlepoint face-down and lay the cardboard frame on top. Fold the triangular canvas flaps over the cardboard and secure with pegs. Check that the inner edges of the frame look neat from the front. You may need to pull the canvas tighter and re-adjust the pegs.

8 Trim the excess canvas and secure the flaps to the cardboard with masking tape. Trim the outer corners of the canvas, fold over the outer flaps (see inset), and secure with tape. Place a picture face-down on the back of the frame, cover with thin cardboard, and secure on three sides with tape.

Golden Birds Mirror

MATERIALS

Paper
Flour and water paste
Gesso
Mirror
Acrylic paints
Thin cardboard
Gold tempera powder
PVA glue
Epoxy putty
Mirror plate
Superglue

EQUIPMENT

Scissors
Housepainter's brush
Pencil
Pair of compasses
Ruler
Artist's brush

THIS LARGE circular mirror frame, made of many layers of papier mâché, is strong and light and exhibits all the interesting irregularities that paper assumes when it gets wet, together with a delicately tattered edge conferred by the *mille-feuille* of paper circles.

Gone are the days when paint has to be matt and flat to be respectable. Here, the broken texture of the paint adds to the visual interest of the frame. The smooth opaque curves of gold seem to float above this choppy surface, all the more refined by contrast. Precision matters not a jot when painting the gold detailing, but an easy, fluent line is all important. It may help to practise first on a piece of paper, just to loosen up your brushstrokes.

The birds decorating this frame are stylized and quite simple but, again, practice will help you achieve sinuous perfection of beak and feather. Finally, the putty surrounding the mirror needs careful moulding to look good – if you doubt your ability to produce even undulations, you could decorate it with a textured stamped pattern, using the tines of a fork.

Aegean Blue
This well-behaved queue of elegant golden birds has Greek origins, while the blue of the frame conjures up images of sun-warmed sea and little fishing boats. Not many mirror frames can do this.

A Mirror with a Message
Though it is not an easy one to decipher. This beautiful rhythmic script on its marbled background was achieved after a great deal of practice for fluency, using a fine sable brush. The putty rim is decorated with beads.

Making and Decorating the Frame

*Elegant golden birds, looking very like the Egyptian sun god,
Ra, parade in a never-ending circle beneath an ultramarine sky.*

Flour and water paste

Thin cardboard

PVA glue

Superglue

Gold tempera powder

Mirror plate

Paper

Mirror

Gesso

Epoxy putty

Acrylic paints

1 *Cut out a large circle of paper, wet it with water to prevent sticking, and lay it on a work surface. Cover it with 20 layers of paper, pasted on with flour and water paste. Leave to dry. The edges of the circle will curl up slightly when drying. When dry, cover both sides of the paper circle with a coat of gesso to provide a smooth surface for decorating with paints.*

2 *When the gesso is dry, draw around the mirror in the centre of the circle with a pencil. Paint the outer edge of the paper circle with phthalo-green acrylic paint.*

3 *Using a pair of compasses, draw a circle on thin cardboard that is larger than the size of the mirror, but smaller than the size of the paper circle. Divide it up into equal segments using the compasses and a ruler. Cut out a circle in the middle — the size of the mirror — and then draw a simple repeating bird outline in each of the outer segments. Cut out the bird template.*

4 Place the template on the paper circle, matching up the central circles. Using an artist's brush dipped in gold tempera powder mixed with water, paint the outline of the birds, using the template as a guide.

5 Paint the inner rim surrounding the mirror area, and the outer rim of the paper circle, with dilute ultramarine acrylic paint. Paint the outer rim with wavy lines, following the shapes of the birds.

6 Add the finer detailing on the bird shapes. Using an artist's brush and gold tempera powder that has been mixed with water, paint on eyes, wings and feathers.

7 When the paint has dried, glue the mirror to the centre of the paper frame using PVA glue. Roll out a long "sausage" of epoxy putty and stick this around the edge of the mirror. Press into place with your thumbs to create a decorative impression (see inset).

8 Paint the epoxy putty rim with gold tempera powder mixed with water. Paint the back of the frame with a coat of ultramarine acrylic paint to seal it. Leave the frame to dry for a couple of hours, then glue a mirror plate to the back of the frame using a strong glue.

Tiny Hooked Frame

MATERIALS

Thin cardboard

Hessian

Assorted fabric strips,
2cm (¾in) wide

Latex adhesive

Clear adhesive

Black felt

Black sewing thread

Drink can ring-pull

Picture glass or mirror

EQUIPMENT

Black marker pen

Embroidery frame

Hook

Scissors

Needle

Pins

ONCE UPON A TIME, country fireside and kitchen rugs were made from the worn out woollens and petticoats accumulated through the year. Cut into strips by one of the younger members of the family, they would be prodded or hooked through a backing of hessian meal bags, a process that occupied a winter and took place annually. These rag rugs would then greet the world at the front door, or bring warmth and cheer to the hearth. They were not made to last forever, and with each passing year would be demoted from parlour to kitchen, finally ending up on the compost heap.

These days, no one has the time or inclination to recycle on this scale, and for most people there is, thankfully, no longer an urgent necessity to make do and mend. However, hooked rags have a texture and personality unlike anything else and are surprisingly easy to make. This witty little frame is made from pieces of man-made fabric acquired at jumble sales – it could be the perfect frame for the family crest. Who knows, you may get hooked yourself, and become a rug addict in time.

Crimplene and Coronets

Hooking rugs is habit-forming – it is one of those soothing, mindless activities that puts problems in a less panicky perspective. Start with an almost instant witty trifle, like this crowned frame, and you will soon find yourself at work on a baronial hearth rug for the east wing.

Rag Time

An irreverent pastiche of pomp and circumstance, these rags are nothing if not regal – a royal purple, lime green and red crown and a fleur-de-lis in dolly mixture fabrics. Just the thing to frame your investiture certificate.

Making and Decorating the Frame

This little frame is a recycler's dream – even the hanging hook is made from a soft drink can ring-pull.

Drink can ring-pull

Black sewing thread

Latex adhesive

Clear adhesive

Black felt

Hessian

Thin cardboard

Assorted fabric strips

1 *Make a cardboard template of the shape of frame you require. Using a marker pen, draw around the template onto the hessian, leaving a border of at least 7.5cm (3in) around the design. Attach the hessian to the embroidery frame.*

2 *Hold a fabric strip underneath the hessian, and push the hook through the hessian from the top. Guide the fabric strip over the hook to create a loop. Pull the hook back up through the hessian, bringing the end of the fabric strip to the top.*

3 *Push the hook down through the hessian again, just next to the first loop, guide the fabric onto the hook and pull through the fabric to the top side to form a loop on the surface (see inset). Pull the strip back until the loop is the required height.*

4 *Continue forming rows of loops to fill the area of the frame. When you reach the end of a fabric strip, bring the end through to the top side and trim to the height of the loops. Change to another colour of fabric when desired.*

5 *Remove the hessian from the frame and lay it face-down on a flat surface. Cut the excess hessian away to leave a border around the frame of 5cm (2in). Using a piece of cardboard, smear a thin layer of latex adhesive over the back of the frame.*

6 *Using scissors, make diagonal cuts in the hessian into the corners of the frame, right up to the hooked area, and fold in the edges, squeezing the corners firmly together. Trim off any excess fabric.*

7 *Make diagonal cuts in the hessian in the central picture area, from corner to corner. Fold each resulting triangular flap back onto the glued area. Leave to dry for 30 minutes.*

8 *Apply a thin layer of clear adhesive onto the back of the frame and place the frame glued-side down on a piece of black felt. Trim the edges of the felt, then carefully cut out the central picture area. Using black sewing thread, slip stitch the felt to the hessian around all the edges to secure. Leave to dry for two hours.*

9 *Cut out a piece of black felt to make a pocket in which to slip the picture glass or mirror. Pin onto the reverse of the frame, centring it over the picture area. Using black sewing thread, blanket stitch the pocket in place, then sew a drink can ring-pull securely onto the back of the frame for the hanging hook (see inset).*

Brilliant Tissue Frame

MATERIALS

Powder paint
Matt acrylic copolymer emulsion
Acid-free plain and decorated tissue paper
Metallic powder
MDF board, 12mm (½in) thick
Acrylic paints
Matt acrylic gel medium
PVA glue
Dark blue emulsion paint
Wooden dowelling
Mirror
Cardboard
Nails
2 hanging hooks
Cord

EQUIPMENT

Housepainter's brush
Artist's brush
Pencil
Jigsaw
Ruler
Hammer

AT FIRST SIGHT, it is impossible to tell what this frame is made of: layer upon layer of rich colour and gold make it as sumptuous as an Indian palace, and as richly textured as scagliola. The opulent irregular surface is held within carefully delineated borders and outlines, a contrast between materials and method that works to their mutual flattery. The components of the frame have a sense of discipline, despite being less than symmetrical, while the shape is singular, with all the arches and complexities of an Islamic gateway. Altogether, this mirror frame achieves the utterly exotic using deceptively simple means.

The secret of this frame's success is the subtle layering of toning colour – there is nothing jarring or glaring in this palette. The effect of using autumnal browns and russets together would be equally successful. For a different look, the frame could be used to show off a wood-blocked motif, printed in cinnabar red on textured cream paper. This is a glorious frame – it would look good against a plain white wall, but is also strong enough to hold its own with paisley and rich ethnic textiles, or lively distemper-type paint.

High-impact Colour
As opulently exotic as the riches of the kasbah, this frame is a tribute to the sizzling potential of paint and tissue paper. A mixture of spontaneity and control governs the build-up of colour, and assembling the collage is a miracle of casual deftness.

Spectrum Exploration
Small changes in shape emphasize the discipline that holds together the kaleidoscope of colour adorning each of these frames. Without discreet but insistent control, these visual symphonies could easily become chaotic cacophony.

70

Making and Decorating the Frame

Customized tissue paper in rich peacock colours make this frame truly sumptuous.

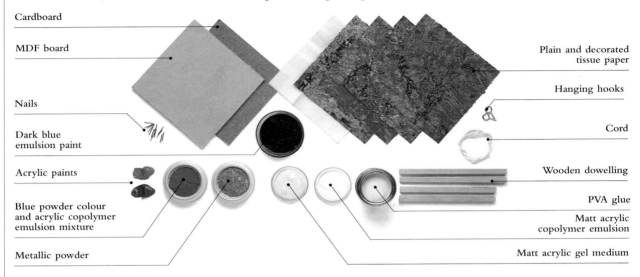

Cardboard

MDF board

Nails

Dark blue
emulsion paint

Acrylic paints

Blue powder colour
and acrylic copolymer
emulsion mixture

Metallic powder

Plain and decorated
tissue paper

Hanging hooks

Cord

Wooden dowelling

PVA glue

Matt acrylic
copolymer emulsion

Matt acrylic gel medium

1 *Mix 10 parts powder colour with 1 part matt acrylic copolymer emulsion and dilute with water to the consistency of single cream. Paint this onto plain tissue paper. When dry, apply paler colours and then metallic powder mixed with matt acrylic copolymer emulsion, rolling the brush over the paper to produce random patterns (see inset). Allow to dry.*

2 *Draw out the shape of the frame on MDF (medium density fibreboard). It can be a simple square or circle, or, as here, an arch with extra pieces jutting out to create added interest. Cut out the frame with a jigsaw.*

3 *Paint areas of blue, purple and green acrylic paint to cover the frame base and allow to dry.*

4 *Draw a rectangle around the inner frame to provide a guideline when gluing on tissue paper. Paste overlapping strips of decorated tissue paper onto the frame using matt acrylic gel medium. Add as many layers as desired for colour and texture.*

5 *Paste more strips of decorated tissue paper in toning colours around the central part of the frame, following the pencil guideline.*

6 *Cut out a second piece of MDF board, larger than the aperture in the frame, to make the inner frame. Cut out a central area for the mirror. Cover this inner frame with decorated tissue paper, pasting it down with matt acrylic gel medium. Fold the tissue back around the inner edge to reveal the mirror area. Glue this inner frame to the outer frame using PVA glue. Leave to dry overnight with a weight on top.*

7 *Paste on further tissue as desired. Here thin side strips and an arch highlight the shape of the frame. Leave to dry before painting the back of the frame with dark blue emulsion paint. When dry, glue four pieces of wooden dowelling around the mirror aperture on the back of the frame. Place the mirror in this dowelling holder, lay backing card on top (see inset) and tack in place with nails (see p.9). Add hanging hooks and cord as required (see p.9).*

Pure Fabrication

MATERIALS

Thick cardboard
Corrugated cardboard
Mirror tile
Masking tape
Cotton fabric
Contrasting
cotton fabric
PVA glue
Embroidery thread
Curtain ring
Braid

EQUIPMENT

Felt-tip pen
Craft knife
Ruler
Scissors
Needle
Pins

THESE FABRIC-COVERED FRAMES would contribute style and opulence to any room. They are perfectly straightforward to make and employ only the most basic of materials – remnants of cloth, pieces of braid and cardboard backing.

There are no limitations of size, shape or colour with this simple technique. Minaret shapes and strong spice colours look magnificent massed among Indian block-printed textiles; classic squares or rectangles suit plainer interiors. A circular chintz frame hung from a bow would look at home in a woman's bedroom, while a triangular frame trimmed with tartan and finished with brass studs would reflect a manly visage without causing embarrassment. Striped ticking would look fresh and clean; bright spots could be a cure for vanity. For a more sumptuous look, experiment with furnishing fabrics – velvet and brocade would lend Renaissance richness to the most humble hall.

Paisley Casbah
This pretty silhouette is reminiscent of the dome of an Indian palace. It is covered with vibrant red paisley cloth, and is finished with decorative braid and a complementary fillet of green fabric.

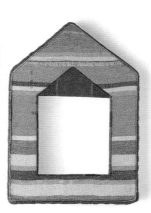

Perfect Adaptability
Toning fabrics make a terrific ensemble. If a multitude of mirrors strikes you as being too much of a good thing, you can echo or contrast the dominant colour of postcards, paintings or photographs to frame them in splendour.

Making and Decorating the Frame

The fabric is attached to the frame using PVA glue. When applying this, take care not to spill it on the surface of the mirror as it may destroy the finish. If you do spill any glue, wipe it off immediately with a damp cloth.

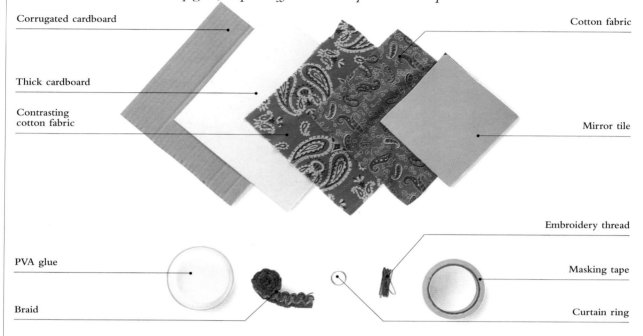

Corrugated cardboard

Thick cardboard

Contrasting cotton fabric

Cotton fabric

Mirror tile

Embroidery thread

PVA glue

Braid

Masking tape

Curtain ring

1 *Make a cardboard template of an arch. Draw around this template on corrugated cardboard and thick cardboard and cut out five shapes: three from corrugated, and two from thick cardboard. Cut a window out of the middle of one of the thick cardboard arches, 12mm (1⁄2 in) smaller all around than the mirror tile.*

2 *Draw around the mirror tile in the middle of one of the corrugated cardboard arches. Using a craft knife, cut out and discard the central piece of cardboard and replace with the mirror tile. Secure the tile with masking tape around all the edges, both on the front and the back of the cardboard.*

3 *Place the two thick cardboard arches on the two contrasting fabrics. Cut around the edges, leaving a 3cm (1¼in) border all around. Set aside one piece of fabric. Cut out a window from the other piece, leaving a 2cm (¾in) border. Snip the fabric into the corners and glue the fabric edges onto the cardboard using PVA glue.*

4 Cut out four strips of contrasting fabric, 4cm (1½in) wide and the length of the mirror tile. Fold each strip in half lengthwise and press to create a neat edge. Using PVA glue, stick each strip to the back of the arch along each edge of the window, overlapping the window slightly so that you can see a narrow strip of the fabric on the right side of the frame.

5 Using embroidery thread, oversew or use blanket stitch to attach a curtain ring to the upper centre of the second piece of fabric. As the ring will be the means of hanging the frame, ensure that the stitching is secure. Remember to stitch around only half of the ring — the other half will be used as the hook.

6 Place the fabric ring-side down. Using PVA glue, stick one corrugated cardboard arch to the remaining thick cardboard arch. Place these glued pieces on top of the fabric with the thick cardboard underneath and wrap the fabric up and over the edges. Snip around the curves of the arch with scissors and glue the fabric in place with PVA glue.

7 Glue the front of the frame to the two remaining corrugated cardboard arches (this is to prevent the mirror coming into contact with the PVA glue as the glue will destroy the silver finish on the mirror). Then sandwich the front and back pieces of the frame together with PVA glue. Place the frame under a heavy weight for several hours to dry thoroughly.

8 Glue decorative braid around the edges of the frame, cutting it to fit at the join. Pin the braid to the frame to hold it in place while it is drying. Remove the pins when the glue has dried. Finally, give the mirror a quick polish to remove any marks.

Gothic Mirror

MATERIALS

Tracing paper
Thick corrugated
cardboard
PVA glue
Newsprint
Wallpaper paste
Black acrylic paint
Wooden batten
Mirror
Mirror adhesive
String
Modelling clay
White emulsion paint
Dark grey
undercoat paint
Dark blue gloss paint
Gold acrylic paint
2 D-ring hangers
and screws

EQUIPMENT

Pencil
Craft knife
Metal ruler
Artist's brush
Housepainter's brush
Sponge
Small dish
Screwdriver

A SPLENDID MIRROR, perfect for Count Dracula to check that no shred of spinach mars his post-prandial canines before going on the razzle, or for the Earl of Essex to adjust his ruff before dallying with Queen Bess. This is a mirror frame with gravitas, whose intricate construction completely supersedes its humble constituents. Despite its considerable size, this mott and bailey of a frame is made from nothing more grandiose than corrugated cardboard, and is surprisingly lightweight and portable.

To reinforce the frame's air of grave antiquity, you could use a mottled and ancient looking glass and distress the paintwork a little. It would look superb in a baronial setting, ideally with crenellated turrets – perhaps a gothic arched hallway, where it could reflect the flickering light from beeswax candles in an iron candlestick. Alternatively, its dignified masculinity and witty relish for pastiche would be quite at home reflecting white walls and designer furniture in a warehouse or loft apartment.

Crenellations in Cardboard
*A russet version of the heraldic mirror, complete with turrets, star, crest
and crenellations. This frame is fiddly to make, but the effort is
handsomely rewarded.*

Making and Decorating the Frame

*A handsome and doughty mirror – plain miraculous when
you realize that it is made of nothing more heroic than
corrugated cardboard.*

Mirror adhesive

Wooden batten

Corrugated cardboard

Newsprint

Thick cardboard

D-ring hangers
and screws

White emulsion paint

Wallpaper paste

PVA glue

Black acrylic paint

Gold acrylic paint

Modelling clay

String

Dark blue gloss paint

Dark grey undercoat paint

1 *Photocopy the templates for the frame (see pp. 92–3) to the required size, and trace templates A to I onto corrugated cardboard. Trace templates K and L onto thick cardboard. Using a craft knife and metal ruler for the straight edges, cut out all the components. You should have a total of 14 pieces cut from corrugated cardboard; the number of pieces cut from thick cardboard – the bricks – will depend on the size of frame you make.*

2 *Using PVA glue, stick the two side pieces (E) onto the front piece (D). Paste strips of torn newsprint over the inside edge using wallpaper paste. Paint the underside of the inside edge with black acrylic paint to prevent the cardboard being reflected in the mirror.*

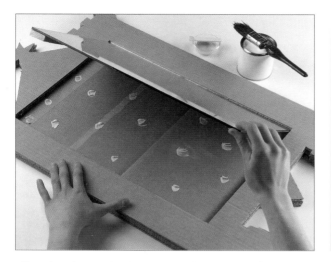

3 *Glue the wooden batten onto the top edge of the mirror back using mirror adhesive. Following the diagram on p.93, assemble the frame. First glue the back pieces (A and B) and centre piece (C) together with PVA glue. Insert the mirror into the centre piece and secure with mirror adhesive. Mark the position of the batten on the back of the frame (this is where the D-ring hangers will be attached).*

4 *Using PVA glue, paste the front piece (D) over the mirror. Attach two steps (I and H) to the base of each side piece. Then glue the battlements (F) to the top of each side piece and the star (G) to the centre top of the frame. Using wallpaper paste, paste three or four layers of torn overlapping pieces of newsprint over the entire mirror frame and allow to dry.*

5 *Add decorative details to the frame. Glue string around the edges of the centre panel. Mould a raised star, raised bosses and a fleur-de-lis (J) from modelling clay and glue in the centre panel. Glue bricks (K and L) down the edges of the two sides, alternating longer and shorter bricks.*

6 *Paint the whole frame with several layers of white emulsion paint to seal. When dry, apply a coat of dark grey undercoat and finally a coat of dark blue gloss paint. Allow to dry.*

7 *Dip a sponge in gold acrylic paint, dab off the excess in a small dish, then dab the sponge over the raised areas of the frame, including the bricks, star, bosses, fleur-de-lis and steps. When dry, screw two D-ring hangers into the back of frame at the position of the wooden batten marked earlier (see inset).*

Gilded Velvet Frame

MATERIALS

35cm (14in) square
of paper

35cm (14in) square
of velvet

2 x 30cm (12in)
squares of fabric

Multi-dyed
rayon thread

Torn strips of blue
and orange silk,
12mm (½in) wide

PVA glue

Mirror tile

2 x 25cm (10in)
squares of corrugated
cardboard

Gold enamel paint

Masking tape

EQUIPMENT

Felt-tip pen

Ruler

Pins

Tailor's chalk

Sewing machine

Small sharp scissors

2 housepainter's
brushes

Craft knife

FOR TOTAL OPULENCE, this is a difficult frame to beat. The raw materials alone look like Aladdin's cave, with a wealth of colour and texture that just makes you want to touch. A hoarder's heaven, this frame is a handsome vindication of a lifetime of collecting scraps and remnants, and could be the glorious final resting place for the ribbons from Christmas packaging that were too wonderful to bin. But you must be bold; the dramatic impact of this frame owes much to the casual imprecision with which it was put together. If you try too hard and measure too exactly, you will end up with something that is prim and fussy.

Using fabric has one great advantage – you can try out different combinations of colour, texture and pattern before you begin. Here the formula is a sumptuous mixture of silks and velvet and there is a definite element of Spanish baroque. You could go seriously over the top and use golden tassels, mirror glass, sequins, braid and beads. Or you might find that plainer, homespun materials suit your home. Let your feeling for the fabrics guide you.

Baroque Splendour

There are times when everybody needs a touch of glamour. The trick is to be unafraid of it. If glamour is your goal, go all out for it with sensuous flocked walls, swathes of sumptuous velvet and golden flowers. Don't apologize, enjoy!

Sumptuous Remnants
There are as many permutations on a theme of satin and silk, velvet and gold as your remnants, research and energy allow. Look to Gothic architecture and Elizabethan costume for inspiration.

Making and Decorating the Frame

*Create a kaleidoscope of colour and texture by using scraps
from the motley collection of fabric in your workbasket to
make a frame. This provides a great way to use up fabric
that is too pretty to throw away.*

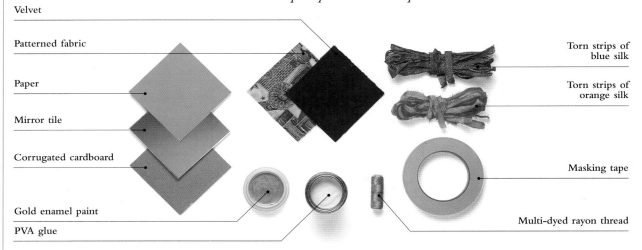

Velvet

Patterned fabric

Paper

Mirror tile

Corrugated cardboard

Gold enamel paint

PVA glue

Torn strips of blue silk

Torn strips of orange silk

Masking tape

Multi-dyed rayon thread

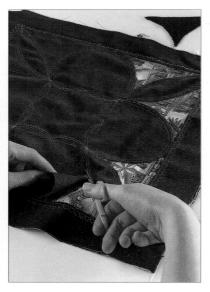

1 *Draw the design of the frame on paper using a felt-tip pen. Here the design is a simple symmetrical pattern of straight lines and curved edges. Pin the wrong side of the velvet square to the right side of one of the patterned fabric squares. Transfer the design from the paper onto the velvet using tailor's chalk (see inset).*

2 *Using a sewing machine threaded with multi-dyed rayon thread, sew two rows of straight stitches around the chalked lines. Stitch around the edge of the square with zigzag stitches.*

3 *Using small scissors, cut out alternating sections of velvet around the outer edge of the square to reveal the patterned fabric beneath. Cut close to the lines of stitching, without cutting the actual threads of the stitches.*

4 *Stitch strips of torn blue silk around the cut edges to outline the velvet. When one strip comes to an end, simply butt up the next strip to this edge and continue stitching.*

5 *Stitch strips of torn orange silk up and down the inner semi-circles of the velvet, to make triangular-shaped blocks. Use either the straight stitch foot or the embroidery foot on the sewing machine. Cut out the centre of the fabric squares.*

6 *Using a housepainter's brush, paint PVA glue over the surface of the fabric. Leave to dry until the glue becomes transparent. Lightly brush gold enamel paint across the surface, so that it just catches the raised areas of the fabric (see inset).*

7 *Using a craft knife, cut out the centre of one square of cardboard the size of the mirror tile. Insert the mirror tile in the aperture and secure with masking tape. Brush PVA glue on the cardboard around the mirror, then place it glue-side down onto the reverse of the painted fabric square, ensuring that the mirror is aligned with the aperture in the fabric. Trim the patterned fabric back to the edge of the cardboard and brush glue over the velvet. Fold the velvet edges over the cardboard, and press them down to secure.*

8 *Glue a square of patterned fabric to the remaining cardboard square, folding the ends over to secure. With fabric facing outwards, glue the two squares of the frame together using PVA glue. If desired, sew a curtain ring onto the back of the frame as a hanging hook (see p. 77).*

Ideas to Inspire

Paper and fabric frames can be extremely inventive and a great excuse to have fun. This section encourages you to be adventurous with hand hooking, machine embroidery, papier mâché, découpage and batik, all of which can form the basis of or add decoration to a frame.

▶ **Padded Silk Frame**
Inspired by Islamic and Indian jewellery, this decorative mirror frame is made from silk, embellished with appliquéd shapes and decorative stitching, then stuffed with wadding (batting) to complete.

▲ **Papier Mâché Aviary**
Featuring stylized bird motifs, this colourful papier mâché frame is made by smoothing paper pulp over a cardboard base, then decorating with crayons for a broken texture.

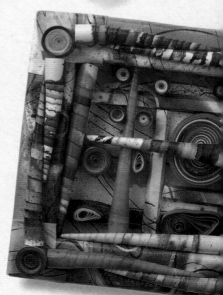

◀ **Hooked Rag Bag**
A delightfully fresh and contemporary approach to the centuries-old tradition of hand-hooking, this decorative mirror frame, made from red, yellow and blue fabric scraps, is good irreverent fun and very quick to make.

► **Gilded for Glamour**
Not a frame for the fainthearted, this splendid creation would bring instant glamour to your home. Made from hardboard and paper pulp, it is decorated with oil-based paint and gold metal transfer.

▲ **Pretty Paperwork**
Painstakingly constructed from pieces of wood glued and pegged together, this highly decorative box cupboard is covered with several layers of ripped paper decorated with oil paints and inks. Copper and brass provide further embellishment.

◄ **Electric Colour**
This multicoloured frame, with its integral central artwork, is made from laminated board covered with watercolour paper that has been dyed with acid-reactive dyes and decorated with penwork. Quilled paper scrolls add extra interest.

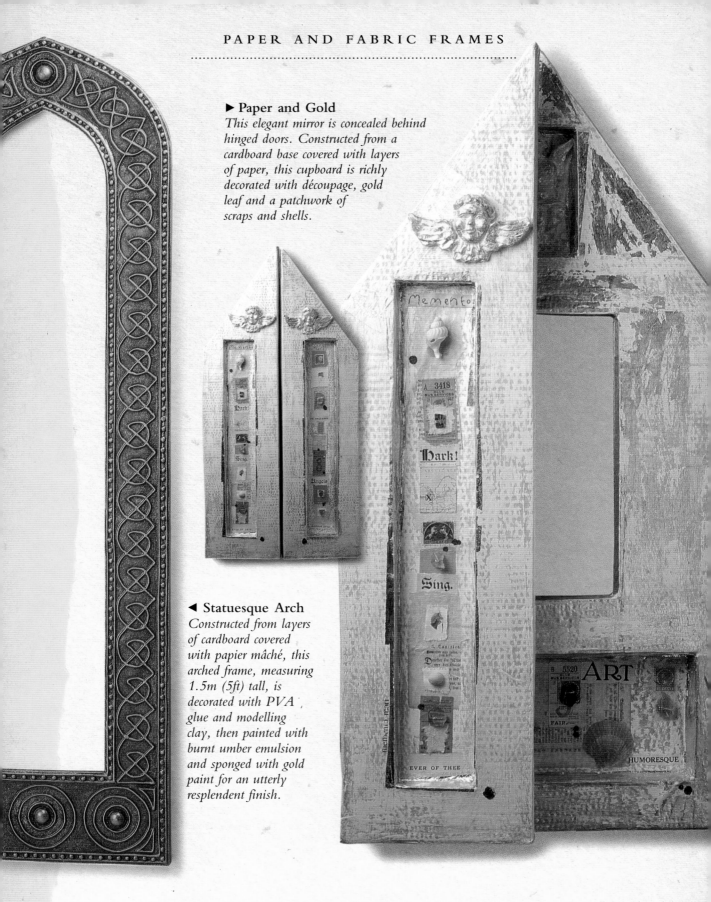

▶ Paper and Gold
This elegant mirror is concealed behind hinged doors. Constructed from a cardboard base covered with layers of paper, this cupboard is richly decorated with découpage, gold leaf and a patchwork of scraps and shells.

◀ Statuesque Arch
Constructed from layers of cardboard covered with papier mâché, this arched frame, measuring 1.5m (5ft) tall, is decorated with PVA glue and modelling clay, then painted with burnt umber emulsion and sponged with gold paint for an utterly resplendent finish.

▼ Edged with Silver

This stylish frame is easily made by gluing decorated handmade papers onto a plain wooden frame. The inner edge of the frame is then gilded with silver leaf and the whole frame is sealed with varnish.

▶ Palladian Classic

Inspired by classical architecture, this impressive arched frame is constructed from corrugated cardboard covered with layers of newsprint, then sponged all over in sombre shades of grey emulsion paint.

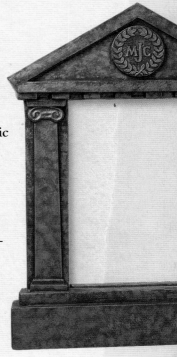

▼ Batik Frame

Using hand-painted fabric for decoration, this wooden frame is first sprayed with car paint, then the batik-dyed fabric is glued in position and the entire frame sealed with clear waterproof varnish.

▲ Wreathed in Ivy

This inventive papier mâché frame is decorated with ivy leaves, each made from several layers of paper glued together and attached to the frame with wire to stand proud.

Templates

Shown here are the templates for four of the projects featured earlier in the book. Enlarge the templates to the required size on a photocopier, keeping all the templates from one project in proportion to each other.

Rustic Chicken Frame
(p. 40)

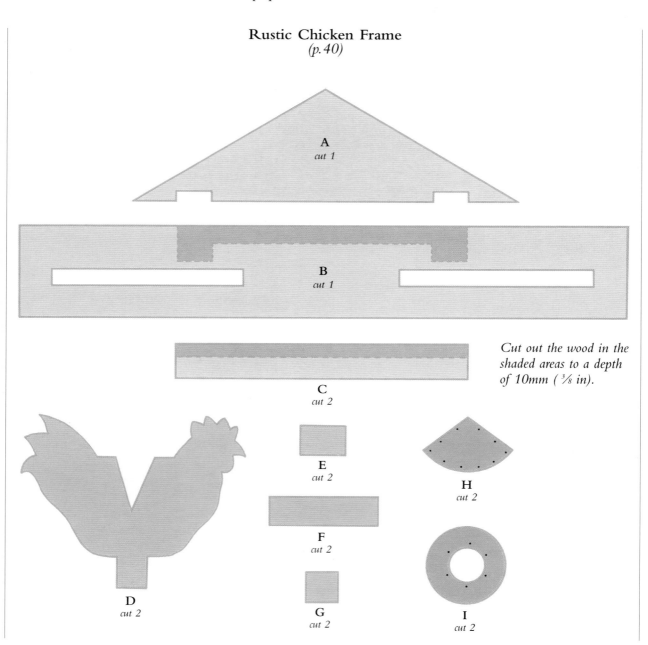

A
cut 1

B
cut 1

Cut out the wood in the shaded areas to a depth of 10mm (⅜ in).

C
cut 2

E
cut 2

H
cut 2

F
cut 2

D
cut 2

G
cut 2

I
cut 2

Baronial Candle Sconce
(p.44)

Folk Stitches
(p.58)

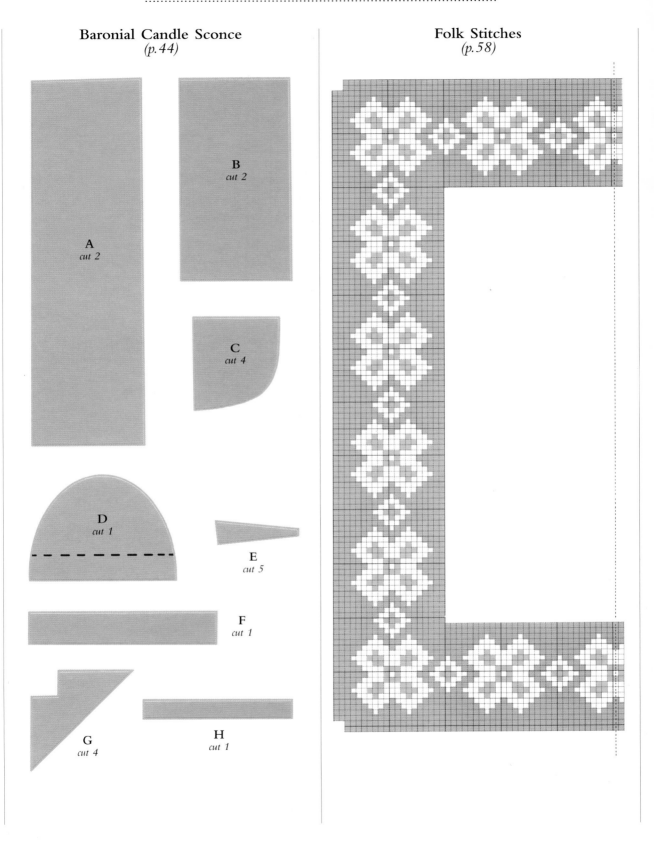

A
cut 2

B
cut 2

C
cut 4

D
cut 1

E
cut 5

F
cut 1

G
cut 4

H
cut 1

Gothic Mirror
(p. 78)

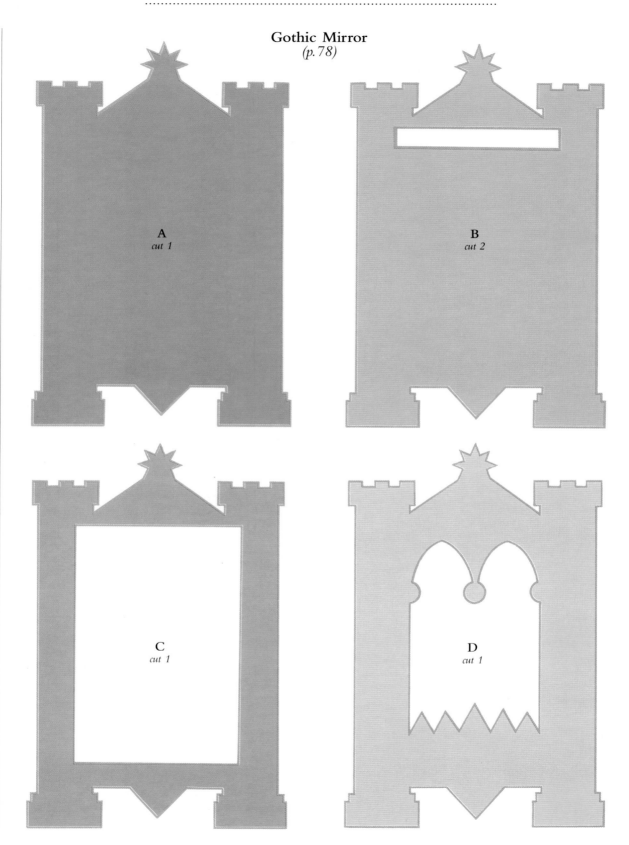

A
cut 1

B
cut 2

C
cut 1

D
cut 1

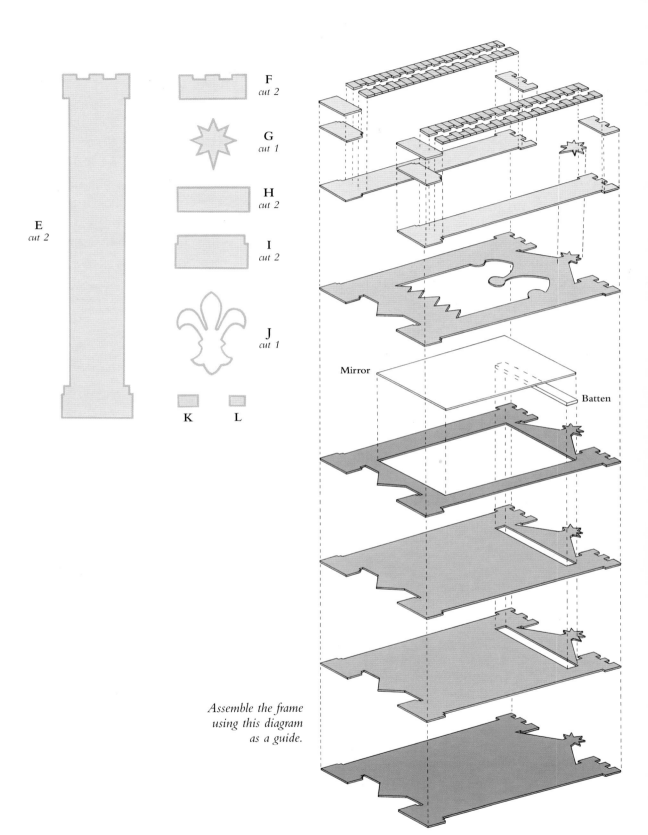

E
cut 2

F
cut 2

G
cut 1

H
cut 2

I
cut 2

J
cut 1

K   **L**

Mirror

Batten

*Assemble the frame
using this diagram
as a guide.*

Contributors

The Author
pp.12-15; pp.20-23

Madeleine Adams
p.86 centre
Tel: 01608 684661
Cobweb Cottage
Stourton Hill
Nr Shipston on Stour
Warwickshire CV36 5HH

Sonia Akow
pp.24-27; p.51 bottom right
Tel: 0171-373 8705
Flat 20
45 Earls Court Square
London SW5 9BY

Clare Bawcutt
p.50 bottom
Tel: 0171-376 8390
32 Glebe Place
Chelsea, London SW3 5JP

Alison Britton
p.89 bottom right
Tel: 01365 324499
The Buttermarket
Down Street
Enniskillen
Co Fermanagh
Northern Ireland BT74 7DU

Patrick Burton
pp.70-73
Tel: 0171-703 3393
3 Urlwin Street
London SE5 0NF

Ann Carter
p.89 bottom centre
Tel: 01993 702335
15 Church Green
Witney
Oxfordshire OX8 6AZ

Martin Cheek
pp.36-39
Tel: 0171-731 0241
53 Pursers Cross Road
Fulham, London SW6 4QY
*Martin Cheek runs weekend mosaic
and ceramic courses; write to the
above address for further details.*

Jason Cleverly
p.48 top
Tel: 0171-703 8517
9a Iliffe Yard
London SE17 3QA

Patricia Crowther
p.49 centre
Tel: 01736 796575
1 Tregenna Villas
Tregenna Terrace, St Ives
Cornwall TR26 2DJ

Hazel Dolby
p.88 bottom right
Tel: 01420 588311
Deanyers Cottage
Hall Lane
Farringdon, Alton
Hampshire GU34 3EA

Amanda Foot
pp.40-43
Tel: 01308 423997
6 Glebe Close
Churchfields, Bridport
Dorset DT6 4DT

Ann Frith
pp.54-57; p.87 bottom right
Tel: 01273 625365
5 Chesham Street
Kemptown, Brighton
East Sussex BN2 1NA

Victor Stuart Graham
p.50 top left
Tel: 01273 203168
78 Montpelier Road
Brighton
East Sussex BN1 3BD

Gigi Griffiths
pp.74-77
Tel: 01273 821341
Basement Flat
35 Norfolk Square
Brighton
East Sussex BN1 2PE

Tony Isseyegh
p.51 centre
Tel: 01422 844559
Unit 6, Bridge Mill
Hebden Bridge
West Yorkshire HX7 7NB

Paul Johnson
p.86 bottom right
Tel: 0161-434 1699
30 Queenston Road, Didsbury
Manchester M20 2NX

Andrea Maflin
p.89 top left
Tel: 0171-284 1224
50 Croftdown Road
London NW5 1EN

Lorna Moffat
pp.82-85
Tel: 01233 638508
38 Canon Woods Way
Kennington, Ashford
Kent TN24 9QY

Helen Musselwhite
pp.28-31; p.51 top right
Tel: 01235 528292
25 Bridge Street
Abingdon
Oxfordshire OX14 3HN

Cleo Mussi
p.49 right
Tel: 0171-498 2727
(Home: 081-785 2433)
Unit 72C
Abbey Business Centre
15-17 Ingate Place
London SW8 3NS

Mary Norden
pp.58-61
Tel: 0171-226 7570
162 Downham Road
London N1 3HL

Sarah Parish
pp.16-19
Tel: 01243 514007
The Workshop
Itchenor Gate Farm
Itchenor, Nr Chichester
West Sussex PO20 7DA

Maxine Pharoah
pp.50-51 top centre
Tel: 01831 340987
Fern Cottage
Rugby Road, Brinklow
Warwickshire CV23 0LY

Mandy Pritty
pp.48-49 bottom
Tel: 0171-249 0038
76 Carysfort Road
London N16 9AP

Trisha Rafferty
p.48 centre
Tel: 01273 327792
18 Tichborne Street
Brighton
East Sussex BN1 1UR

Lizzie Reakes
pp.66-69; p.86 bottom left
Tel: 0181-840 7579
68 Oaklands Road, Hanwell
Ealing, London W7

Carolyn Sansbury
pp.62-65
Tel: 01273 735804
12b Powis Square
Brighton
East Sussex BN1 3HG

Jackie Shelton
p.88 top right
Tel: 01785 850859
3 Railway Cottages
Badnall Wharf, Eddleshall
Staffordshire ST2 6LG

Claire Sowden
p.86 top right
Tel: 01252 870334
6 Bramling Avenue
Yateley, Camberley
Surrey GU17 7NX

Eleanor Staley
pp.78-81; p.88 left; p.89 top right
Tel: 01684 574392
32 St Ann's Road
Great Malvern
Worcestershire WR14 4RG

Alison Start
pp.44-47
Tel: 01273 674809
12 Arnold Street
Brighton
East Sussex BN2 2XT

James Taylor
pp.32-35
Tel: 01273 609207
Flat 1
78 Dyke Road
Brighton
East Sussex BN1 3JD

Juliet Walker
p.87 top left
Tel: 01590 675135
79a Southampton Road
Lymington
Hampshire SO41 9GH

Steve Wright
p.49 top
Tel: 0181-299 3164
45 Melbourne Grove
East Dulwich
London SE22 8RG

Index

Acknowledgements

This book owes just about everything to the talent and generosity of the many frame-makers whose work it shows. Craftspeople are an endangered species and eke out a precarious living. I hope this book will tempt you to share the satisfaction and fun that they enjoy, but it should not prevent you from buying their work – skilful, different and inspiring – wherever you can lay hands on it; fortunately, there are some excellent craft fairs around of late – the Craft Movement, Dazzle, and Chelsea Craft Fair, for example. Of the many galleries crammed with talent, the Bluecoat School in Liverpool and Craftdirect in Brighton have been particularly helpful and inspiring.

The people who turned the ravishing raw material into a book were Clive Streeter who took the pictures and personifies patience, endurance and ingenuity; Marnie Searchwell who made sure they looked good and contributed a sure hand and fastidious quality control; Ali Edney, the ariel of stylists, who sped over unimaginable distances in her quest for props; and Heather Dewhurst who did the most difficult thing of all – composed the haiku of step-by-step instructions, along with some mettlesome editing.

Stuart Stevenson of the excellent eponymous shop let us make free with his paints and papers. Roger Bristow effected one or two daring rescues, and Sarah Hoggett kept the whole unruly caravan behaving as it ought. Finally, Kate Haxell and Claire Worthington contributed more than they thought.

The following companies kindly loaned props for photography:

The Bath House
Liberty PLC, Regent Street,
London W1R 6AH;
Tel: 0171-734 1234.
Soap dish, soap, snails and chrome metal bottles featured on p.55; frosted glass bottles featured on p.59.

City Hardware
6-10 Goswell Road,
London EC1M 7AA;
Tel: 0171-253 4095.
Hardware.

Czech & Speake
244-254 Cambridge Heath Road, London E2 9DA;
Tel: 0181-980 4567.
Glass shelf with chrome brackets featured on p.55.

Farrow & Ball
33 Uddens Trading Estate,
Wimborne, Dorset BH21 7NL;
Tel: 01202 876141.
'Stone White' matt emulsion paint featured on p.21.

Foxell and James Ltd
57 Farringdon Road,
London EC1M 3JH;
Tel: 0171-405 0152.
Specialist paints and pigments.

C.R. Frost & Son Ltd
60-62 Clerkenwell Road,
London EC1M 5PX;
Tel: 0171-253 0315.
Specialist hardware.

Liberty PLC
Regent Street,
London W1R 6AH;
Tel: 0171-734 1234.
Haberdashery.

Osborne and Little
49 Temperley Road,
London SW12 8QE;
Tel: 0181-675 2255.
Wallpaper featured on pp.13 and 79.

Stuart R. Stevenson
68 Clerkenwell Road,
London EC1M 5QA;
Tel: 0171-253 1693.
Artist's materials.

The V & N
29 Replingham Road,
London SW18 5LT;
Tel: 0181-874 4342.
Bead necklace featured on p.59; two French candelabra featured on p.83.

Watts of Westminster
7 Tufton Street,
London SW1P 3QE;
Tel: 0171-222 2893.
Cotton chenille featured on p.83.